The Worship-Driven Life

THE REASON WE WERE CREATED

A. W. TOZER
EDITED BY
JAMES L. SNYDER

MONARCH
BOOKS

Oxford, UK & Grand Rapids, Michigan, USA

Copyright © by Lowell Tozer, 2008.
The right of A. W. Tozer to be identified as author of this work has been
asserted by him in accordance with the Copyright, Designs and Patents
Act 1988.

First published in the UK in 2008 by Monarch Books
(a publishing imprint of Lion Hudson plc),
Wilkinson House, Jordan Hill Road, Oxford OX2 8DR
Tel: +44 (0) 1865 302750   Fax: +44 (0) 1865 302757
Email: co-ed@lionhudson.com
www.lionhudson.com

ISBN: 978 1 85424 877 0

Distributed by:
Marston Book Services Ltd, PO Box 269, Abingdon, Oxon OX14 4YN

Unless otherwise stated, Scripture quotations are taken from the Holy
Bible, New International Version, © 1973, 1978, 1984 by the International
Bible Society. Used by permission of Hodder & Stoughton Ltd. All right
reserved.

This book has been printed on paper and board independently
certified as having come from sustainable sources.

British Library Cataloguing Data
A catalogue record for this book is available from the British Library.

Printed and bound in Wales by Creative Print & Design.

Contents

Introduction by James L. Snyder:
    A. W. Tozer – A Heart for Worship   7

1. The Tragedy of Human Depravity   21
2. Searching for Lost Human Identity   37
3. Discovering the Heart of Human Nature   51
4. Paths in the Wrong Direction   63
5. Religion versus Worship   77
6. Seekers after Truth   89
7. What Came First: Workers or Worshipers?   99
8. The Components of True Worship   113
9. The Mystery of True Worship   127
10. The Natural Dwelling Place of God   139
11. The Worthy Object of Worship   153
12. The Authenticity of Ownership   163
13. The Lord of our Worship   173
14. Maintaining a Vibrant Worship Lifestyle   183

Introduction
by James L. Snyder

A. W. Tozer – A Heart for Worship

For more than forty-four years, Aiden Wilson Tozer served as a minister in the Christian and Missionary Alliance. His most prominent ministry was thirty-one years at the Southside Alliance Church in Chicago, often referred to as 'that citadel of fundamentalism'. His ministry, however, went beyond the confines of a denomination. He served as a voice to the entire body of Christ. His books and articles were eagerly read and his conference ministry attended with great expectation. Rarely did he disappoint those who knew him. If you were looking for formula Christianity, you were disappointed with him. If you were interested in what he referred to as 'feel-good Christianity', you were greatly disappointed.

During his life, Tozer earned a reputation for many things: an outspoken critic of the religious scene, an outstanding preacher, editor of a leading Christian periodical and author of several devotional classics. The real focus, however, of his daily life centered on the worship of God. Nothing else so occupied his mind and life. This worship of God was not something tacked on to a busy schedule. It became the one great passion of his life. Everything revolved around his personal worship of God.

Tozer paid the price for this lifestyle of worship. Many, even in his own family, did not understand him and his insistence on being alone. Some even regarded him as a bit odd, but what others thought of him did not trouble him in the least. His primary business was the worship of God. Nothing else mattered.

To appreciate the ministry of Tozer you must comprehend his passion for worship. If not, you will most likely misunderstand not only his words but his actions as well. He was completely committed to this one solemn activity and pursued it with all the passion he had. Tozer's ideas regarding worship were hammered into a conviction that governed his life and ministry. 'Worship,' Tozer explained, 'is to feel in your heart and express in some appropriate manner a humbling but delightful sense of admiring awe and astonished wonder and overpowering love in the presence of that most ancient Mystery, that majesty which philosophers call the First Cause but which we call Our Father Which Art in Heaven.'

Tozer walked to the beat of a different drummer, but it was not simply because he was a rebel. That may have been a small part of it, but the main factor was his complete sellout to Jesus Christ. Family, friends, even the ministry had to take a back seat to this yearning of his. Perhaps his essay 'The Saint Must Walk Alone' explains to a certain degree his idea of true spirituality. His focus in life was on the person of Jesus Christ and he would do everything within his powers to sharpen that focus. All his spiritual energies and disciplines were directed along that singular path. Consequently, to a certain degree he was difficult to live with, not because he was demanding or irascible but because he simply was focused on God.

At times, he would come to the family dinner table, especially after the children had left, and not speak a word. Not because he was mad at anyone; he was focused on God and would not break that focus even for fellowship around the table with friends and family. Tozer did not spend too much time working on his social graces – probably the one glaring weakness in his character. Yet doing the work he believed God had called him to demanded much time away from people, shut up alone with God.

Tozer daily cultivated the ability to focus on God. He would quiet his heart, and out of that quietness would come adoration and worship for the Triune Godhead.

Often, at conferences, Tozer seemed preoccupied. He was always musing on some aspect of God. He once claimed that he had dreams of God, so much were his thoughts directed toward the Godhead. Although quite knowledgeable on a variety of subjects and possessing strong opinions on many of them, in later life Tozer increasingly became disengaged from them. His focus on God was getting sharper. The 'art' of worship increasingly engaged his time.

The lessons Tozer learned in worship he generously shared with all who would listen. His preaching and writing were simply the clear declarations of what he had experienced in his private sessions with God. Emerging from his prayer closet, dripping with the fragrance of the presence of God, he was eager to report all he had witnessed. After such a sermon during his Chicago ministry, one person in the congregation observed, 'He out-Davided David.'

Few writers got to the heart of a subject as quickly as Tozer. He bypassed the trivial and concentrated on those essential ingredients important to our walk with God. In this series, he bares his soul on the one great obsession of his life: worship. Many have written about worship, but I believe Tozer surpasses them all in simple passion and supreme purpose. A reader coming away from this book will not only understand worship but also experience it in his or her own heart.

You may not always agree with him, but you will always know what he believes and why. He says, 'This will be the best teaching in my ministry, comparing myself with myself.' The ensuing messages prove Tozer to be the prophet his reputation suggests.

'I want to deliver my soul as a prophet of God to the people, and to explain why we were created and why we are here, not to the satisfaction of the immediate appetite only but to something bigger, grander and more eternal, that we might worship God and enjoy Him forever.'

Throughout this book, Dr Tozer systematically presents his teaching on a subject close to his heart. Nowhere will anybody find a more fully developed thesis on worship with such sanctified passion. Tozer was one of the first in evangelical circles to call attention to this neglected Bible doctrine. He issued a clarion call for Christians to return to their first love. Now that the pendulum has swung to the other extreme in the evangelical church, this teaching is as needed today as when

Tozer first preached it. Many people are interested in the subject of worship, but most books focus on technology and performance. Here is a book deeply rooted in Bible doctrine and historical writings which focuses on presence, the presence of God. One of the great aspects of this book is how Tozer blends Scripture with some of the great devotional writers throughout history. Many refer to these as mystics, and Tozer is responsible for introducing these great saints to Protestants and evangelicals. The book is well seasoned with these great saints of the past and their Spirit-inspired writings.

A close study of Tozer's ministry will warrant the simple conclusion that his ministry was not just cranking out sermons, articles and editorials. He always had something significant to report. His entire ministry was marked with this distinction. He firmly believed that his labor must flow from a life of worship. Any work that does not flow from worship is unacceptable to God. And, after all, it is God we are trying to please, not people.

Throughout his long ministry, Tozer never became entangled in social or political issues. Not that he did not have an opinion on these subjects, for he did. His conviction was that he was responsible to stick to the great essentials of life. That is why his writings are just as fresh and relevant today as when they were first published. He believed that certain things never change, whatever the generation. He kept to those fundamentals, and you either loved Tozer or hated him. While other ministers were becoming involved in political issues, Tozer contented himself with preaching about God.

This was his passion.

In this book on worship, Tozer's purpose is twofold: to deliver his soul on a subject close to his heart and to inspire others to cultivate a spirit of worship in daily living. Tozer lays a solid foundation, and once a person has read this book they will go on to develop a lifestyle in which worship dominates their life. Nobody reading this book all the way through will ever be the same again, especially when it comes to their personal worship of God.

Often, when in a thoughtful mood, Tozer confided to a friend, 'My ambition is to love God more than anyone of my generation.' Whatever he meant by that, it is evident that he possessed a passion for God that controlled everything in his life. Some evidence exists suggesting he achieved his goal more than he imagined.

The first book he authored that brought him to the attention of the Christian public was the classic *The Pursuit of God*. The last book was *The Knowledge of the Holy*. Tozer lived between these two books. He lived a lifestyle of worship and nothing else truly mattered to him. He sacrificed family, friends and reputation in his pursuit of God.

Tozer's criticism of entertainment within the church made him quite infamous during his lifetime. His high view of worship caused him to lash out mercilessly at times. Worship was to be pure and untainted by worldly things. In his mind, the two were opposed to each other. When someone suggested that singing a hymn was a form of entertainment, it provoked Tozer's fury. Some of his most eloquent denunciations were in this direction. He was justly concerned about the inroads worldliness was making into the church, and its effect upon Christians. He was especially adamant about the contemporary evangelism methods that many were advocating. He felt they lowered the standards of the church and he was dead set against them.

His comments at times are sharp but this is because of his deep love for the church and the fellowship of God's people. He did not relish the idea of any compromise with the message or the spirit of New Testament Christianity. He truly believed that the church of Jesus Christ had a viable message for the world and was anxious that the message should not be mixed or diluted. Desperate times require strong medicine. And Tozer felt the church was backing away from its strong medicine and becoming adjusted to the world around it, a phrase he detested.

He aptly described his philosophy when he said, 'I believe everything is wrong until God sets it right.' This is where he began and, from that position, he proclaimed freedom through the Lord Jesus Christ.

Tozer once wrote a booklet, 'The Menace of the Religious Movie', in which he set forth in irresistible logic his conviction on this whole matter of entertainment in the church. The opinions are strong yet backed by biblical principles. Not only must the message please God but the methods of getting that message out must please God and be compatible with the character and nature of God. He continually ridiculed the idea that 'new days demand new ways'.

To appreciate fully Tozer's criticism of entertainment, his idea of worship must be examined. He firmly believed that entertainment would undermine Christian worship and put the church in jeopardy, a thought abhorrent to Tozer. The integrity of the church, as Tozer saw it, was in danger of being compromised by the introduction of 'things' into the sanctuary. His ideas of music, prayer, evangelism and missions sprang from the imperative of worship within the Christian community.

The legacy of Tozer is in the area of the majesty of God. Whatever else Tozer did, his supreme desire was to exalt the Lord Jesus Christ as simply as possible. He tried to set before his generation the importance of certain virtues such as simplicity and solitude. And to turn the attention of the young preachers, for he had great influence among them, away from sham and pretense and all kinds of flesh that would creep into church politics. Getting alone with your Bible and a hymnbook was highly recommended by Tozer. It was this intimacy with God that made his ministry what it became and is remembered now.

Also, a significant aspect of his legacy is spiritual insight. Tozer saw into the nature of things so deeply that it burdened him. He once made the remark that, if you wanted to be happy, you should not pray for discernment. Tozer had the gift of spiritual discernment. He could see through to the very nature of things and see beyond the present action to the inevitable results in the years to come. He could see that the way the evangelical church of his day was going meant it would soon be in serious

14

spiritual trouble. His message was always to turn back to God, despite the inconvenience or cost. He urged churches to forget the Madison Avenue techniques, the strategies of the world and their programs and priorities. He advocated a life of sacrifice, self-denial and service for Christ.

During his lifetime, Tozer was widely recognized as a spokesman for God. His insight into spiritual matters was penetratingly accurate. He was widely read, but rarely followed. Those who did have the courage to follow discovered, to their delight, spiritual realities surpassing anything this world has to offer. Once seen, it is difficult to go back to the religious boredom of the average Christian.

Tozer usually directed his ministry toward the common Christian, not the average. His message could be understood by the common person in the pew but the average Christian, delighting in mediocrity, took no delight in his pronouncements and spiritual ardor. It was once said of St Augustine, Bishop of Hippo, that he was a radical Christian. Such could be said of A. W. Tozer.

In his prayers, Tozer never feigned a sanctimonious posture but maintained a continuous sense of God that enveloped him in reverence and adoration. His one daily exercise was the practice of the presence of God, pursuing him with all his time and energy. To him, Jesus Christ was a daily wonder, a recurring astonishment, a continual amazement of love and grace.

'If you major on knowing God,' Tozer once wrote, 'and cultivate a sense of his presence in your daily life, and do what Brother Lawrence advises, "Practice the presence of God" daily and seek to know the Holy Spirit in the Scriptures, you will go a long way in serving your generation for God. No man has any right to die until he has served his generation.'

Correct doctrine was not enough for Tozer. 'You can be', Tozer delighted in saying, 'straight as a gun barrel theologically and as empty as one spiritually.' His emphasis was always on a personal relationship with God; a relationship so real, so personal and so overpowering as to utterly captivate a person's full attention. He longed for what he termed a 'God-conscious soul', a heart aflame for God.

The lack of spirituality among men and women today is embarrassingly evident. Tozer zeroed in on one of the primary causes. 'I am convinced', Tozer said, 'that the dearth of great saints in these times even among those who truly believe in Christ is due at least in part to our unwillingness to give sufficient time to the cultivation of the knowledge of God.' He went on to develop this further: 'Our religious activities should be ordered in such a way as to leave plenty of time for the cultivation of the fruits of solitude and silence.'

There were times when Tozer stood alone on certain issues, which never intimidated him in the least. He never concerned himself about who stood with him on any issue. His concern was always with the truth. He was fearless in his denunciation, which made enemies rather quickly. He once criticized a popular new Bible translation. 'Reading that new translation', opined Tozer, 'gave me the same feeling a man might have if he tried to shave with a banana.'

People waited upon Tozer's ministry with expectancy, knowing that they would hear old truths robed in fresh and sparkling, and sometimes startling, expressions. Tozer once said, 'Years ago I prayed that God would sharpen my mind and enable me to receive everything he wanted to say to me. I then prayed that God would anoint my head with the oil of the prophet so I could say it back to the people. That one prayer has cost me plenty since, I can tell you that.'

Raymond McAfee, Tozer's assistant for more than fifteen years, regularly went to Tozer's study each Tuesday, Thursday and Saturday morning for a half hour of prayer. Often, as McAfee entered, Tozer would read aloud something he had recently been reading – it might be from the Bible, a hymnal, a devotional writer or a book of poetry. Then he would kneel by his chair and begin to pray. At times, he prayed with his face lifted upward. Other times he would pray totally prostrated on the floor, a piece of paper under his face to keep him from breathing carpet dust.

McAfee recalls one especially memorable day: 'Tozer knelt by his chair, took off his glasses and laid them on the chair. Resting on his bent ankles, he clasped his hands together, raised his face with his eyes closed and began: "O God, we are before you." With that, there came a rush of God's presence that filled the room. We both worshiped in silent ecstasy and wonder and adoration. I've never forgotten that moment, and I don't want to forget it.'

In prayer, Tozer would shut out everything and

everyone and focus on God. His mystic mentors taught him that. They showed him how to practice daily the presence of God. He learned the lesson well.

The primary emphasis of Tozer's ministry in preaching and writing was on this area of worship. To him, worship is the Christian's full time occupation. Nothing should be allowed to interfere with or diminish this sacred duty of the believer. According to Tozer, whatever did not flow naturally if not spontaneously out of our worship was not authentic and was at best contrived. Only cunning works of silver and gold should be offered to God.

Almost as a lone voice in his generation, Tozer stressed the need for a drastic reform of worship both personally and congregationally. Our ideas of worship must be in complete harmony with the revealed Word of God.

During the 1950s, Tozer found a kindred spirit in a plumber from Ireland, Tom Haire, a lay preacher. Haire became the subject of seven articles Tozer wrote for *Alliance Life* entitled 'The Praying Plumber from Lisburn', later reissued as a booklet. Two men could hardly have been more different, yet their love for God and their sense of his worth drew them together.

Once, while Haire was visiting Chicago, Tozer's church was engaged in a night of fasting and prayer. Haire joined them. In the middle of the night, he got thirsty and went out for a cup of tea. Some church members felt that Tom, by so doing, had 'yielded to the flesh'. Tozer disagreed. He saw in that act the beautiful liberty Tom enjoyed in the Lord.

Just before Haire was to return to his homeland, he stopped by Chicago to say goodbye.

'Well, Tom,' Tozer remarked, 'I guess you'll be going back to Ireland to preach.'

'No,' Tom replied in his thick Irish brogue. 'I intend to cancel all appointments for the next six months and spend that time preparing for the judgment seat of Christ while I can still do something about it.'

It was an attitude not uncharacteristic of Tozer himself.

If this book drives you to your knees in penitential worship before God and encourages you to withdraw from the rat race of religious life and focus on your birthright of worship, it will be well worth the pains of publication. And A. W. Tozer, '[…] being dead, yet speaks'.

CHAPTER 1

The Tragedy of Human Depravity

In the beginning, God created Adam and Eve, placing them in the beautiful garden east of Eden. We have only a little glimpse into the beauty of that mysterious and wondrous world. All we know is that God created it and afterwards said, 'It is good.' This meant that all creation was in absolute harmony with God, and fulfilling its ordained purpose.

Perhaps it would be correct to suggest that many people in their frantic pursuit of life have forgotten the purpose of their creation from God's point of view. Keep in mind that whatever God created, he created for his purpose and pleasure (Revelation 4:11). To entertain the idea that God would do anything capriciously or without purpose is to misunderstand the nature of God completely.

After God had created everything else, he said with a smile on his face, 'I'll make me a man.' Stooping down, he took up the clay from the bed of the river, shaped it and worked on it like a nanny bending over her baby. He shaped and formed human beings and blew into their nostrils the breath of life, and they became living souls. God stood the first man on his feet and said, 'Look around, this is all yours, and look at me, I am yours, and I'll look at you and I'll see in your face the reflection of my own glory. That is your end, that is why you were created, that you might worship me and enjoy me and glorify me and have me as yours forever.'

God then put Adam in a deep sleep and out of his ribs formed woman, whom Adam called Eve. Together they were created with one purpose.

God's purpose in creating Adam and Eve is summed up in what they could do for God that nothing else in the whole creation could do. They had an exclusive on God shared by no other part of God's creation. Unlike everything else in this mystic and marvelous world of God's creation, Adam and Eve could worship God and God anticipated that worship. In the cool of the day, God came down and walked with Adam and Eve in the garden of Eden where they joyously offered their reverence and adoration. Nowhere do we read that God came down and hugged a tree or walked with any animal or plant he had created, nor did he talk to any of the animals. Only Adam and Eve were able to provide the fellowship God desired. It was their unique purpose, shared by nothing else in all of God's creation.

Thinking of those occasions when God walked with them in the cool of the day in the garden, I wonder what they talked about. The weather was ideal, Adam and Eve enjoyed perfect health, and sports had not been invented. Obviously, it was a fellowship based on compatibility between both parties. Something in human beings responded to the presence of God like nothing else in all God's creation. God created people in his own image, and out of that flowed the marvelous dynamic of worship. Adam and Eve's unique purpose in the garden was to bring pleasure, joy and fellowship to God, which is the foundation of all genuine worship.

Everything in the garden was in perfect harmony and symmetry. Then God withdrew for a moment, and while he was gone, that old evil one, the dragon who is called Satan, came and sowed poisonous seed in the minds of Adam and Eve. Consequently, they rebelled against God and his purpose for them. When Adam and Eve crossed the line, immediately God knew the fellowship was broken, for God knows all things.

Also, for Adam and Eve there was a terrific sense of disorientation, resulting in spiritual amnesia. They looked at themselves for the first time and saw themselves in a different light. They saw their nakedness and, in a state of spiritual disorientation, gathered fig leaves to hide this nakedness. Thus was born religion; Fig-Leaf Religion. Religion always focuses on the externals and Adam and Eve were consumed with their outward condition. They had lost the focus of their inward beauty and purpose and no longer satisfied the criteria of fellowship with their Creator.

When God came as usual for fellowship, Adam and Eve were nowhere to be found, and God sought them among the trees in the garden, calling out to Adam, 'Where are you?'

God called out to the man who had fled from him and hidden among the trees of the garden. Adam heard the voice of the Lord in the cool of the day, as before, but he was confused. Why was God coming to Eden eastward;

what was he doing there? He was coming for his customary time with Adam when Adam should worship, admire and adore the God who made him.

Adam, shamefaced, came crawling out from behind some tree.

God asked, 'What did you do?'

Adam regretfully replied, 'We ate of the forbidden fruit.' Then, to justify his actions, he said this: 'But it was the woman you gave me.'

God turned to the woman. 'What did you do?' Immediately she put the blame on the serpent.

Already they had learned to blame somebody else for the condition of their souls. This blaming of someone else for all our iniquities is one of the great evidences of sin and the forerunner of religion.

Something happened, changing the whole scenario, hijacking and barring humanity from the knowledge of God. Adam and Eve, in that perfect environment and with their one supreme purpose of worshiping God, rebelled against their purpose, which resulted in what theologians call the fall of man, or depravity.

Our world is full of tragedy because of this great overwhelming cosmic tragedy back in the garden. Repercussions still vibrate in contemporary society.

The burning question needing an answer is: what was the tragic consequence of this fall? Why does this matter for us today, and why should we inquire into it?

Some say the fall is the source of all the problems plaguing humanity down through the years. Some point to the proliferation of disease as a direct outcome. Others point to all the hatred infecting humanity throughout the centuries: nation rising against nation, kingdom against kingdom, and holocausts that have happened periodically throughout history. No generation has escaped such hatred and anger. However, these are short-term effects and simply consequences, not representing the real tragedy of the fall.

So what was the real tragedy of that dreadful cosmic rupture that was forever to affect humankind? The real tragedy in the garden of Eden was that Adam and Eve lost their purpose. They forgot who they were; they did not know where they were; they did not understand where they came from or what they were there for. They forgot the purpose of their existence. Though they tried their best to shake off this moral fog, they could not, for no matter what they did it would not shake off. Therefore, hand in hand, they made their way out into the world, not knowing where they were going. Humanity still wanders in this moral and spiritual wilderness.

They suffered from what I will refer to as 'spiritual amnesia'.

This spiritual morass is illustrated, as is often the case, in the physical world. A man wakes up in the hospital only to discover he has been in a coma for about a week. He does not know how he got there or why he is there. He does not know where he is; in fact, he cannot even remember his name. He is told that over a week ago he encountered muggers, who beat him severely, robbing him of everything including his identity. Anything to tell who he was or why he was in the city was stripped from him. The doctors diagnosed him with amnesia. It is a real problem because the man has no memory of what happened to him. He has lost all perspective on his life, not knowing even his own name making him vulnerable to people he does not know.

This identity crisis is a serious condition and, thankfully, for many people it is only temporary. With the diligent work and patient help of the medical staff, memory can be restored. But, until he regains his memory, he has lost all purpose in life and must rely on others to help him define his purpose.

This is the way it is spiritually. Because the enemy of their souls has mugged humanity, robbing them of their identity, men and women wander around in a spiritual and moral fog not knowing who they are, what they are or where they are going. This is exactly where humanity is today. We have a strange spiritual amnesia and cannot remember who we are or why we are here, and look around for some explanation of our existence. Unfortunately, men and women suffering from this seek answers from anyone offering some hope. Too often, they get the wrong answers from those with less credible integrity, not to mention a personal agenda.

Ask a young university graduate, 'Bob, why are you here?'

'I want to get married, I'd like to make money and I'd like to travel.'

'But listen, Bob, those are short-sighted things. You will do them and then you will get old and die. What is the big overriding purpose of your life?'

Looking rather strange, Bob might say, 'I don't know whether I have any purpose in life.'

This is the condition of the world today, everywhere and in every culture. From the universities to the coalmines, people do not know why they are here. People have a strange moral and spiritual amnesia and do not know their purpose in life, why they were created or what they have been sent to do. Consequently, lives are filled with confusion and people are reaching out for any explanation, hence the proliferation of religions in our world. Religion addresses only humanity's external condition, not our internal confusion.

In spite of this confusion, we try to get around somehow. We travel, play golf, drive cars, eat, sleep and look at beautiful things, but they are all short-sighted aspects of our life.

The enemy of human souls has successfully sabotaged this search for moral and spiritual identity. He does everything within his extensive power to prevent us from discovering who and what we are. Defiantly, knowing our purpose, he stands between us and dares us to cross his line. He offers everything and anything to keep us from finding the right solution. Unfortunately, he has many takers.

Where in the world can we find any answer to this dilemma? What authority in this world can bring us to an understanding of why we are here?

Fortunately for us, the Bible is such an authority, and explains to us why we are here.

I desire to deliver my soul as a prophet of God and

27

explain from the Bible why we were created and why we are here. It may not satisfy the temporary needs at the time, but will satisfy something bigger, grander and more eternal. That biblically defined purpose is that we might worship God and enjoy him forever. Apart from that, we have no other purpose and, short of that, we wander in a spiritual disorientation that takes us farther from finding our created purpose.

God never does anything without a good purpose behind it. God is intelligent because intellect is an attribute of deity. This intellect is seen in every aspect of creation. Nothing in creation is without meaning even if we do not see or understand the meaning at the time.

Deep within the heart of every person is an insatiable longing to know this purpose of life, which, I contend, is an indication of the residue of memory prior to the fall in the garden of Eden. Men and women strive to know the 'why' of everything. They express a legitimate concern and pose an important question demanding a satisfactory answer. The problem is, most people get the wrong answer to their inquiry.

But there is a good and legitimate answer to this query, summed up in the following scriptures: 'My heart is stirred by a noble theme as I recite my verses for the king.' 'The king is enthralled by your beauty; honor him, for he is your Lord' (Psalm 45:1, 11).

And I could go farther into the Psalms: 'Come, let us bow down in worship, let us kneel before the LORD our Maker' (Psalm 95:6).

Additionally, I could turn to many more passages

of sacred Scripture that offer to all mankind a call to worship. It is the echo of the voice of worship telling us why we were born; that we might worship God and enjoy him forever. Informing us that we are to glorify him forever and, above all other creatures, know, admire, love and adore the triune God. To give to God that which he desires.

In our Bibles, we read of those who worship God day and night in the Temple and never ceased chanting, 'Holy, holy, holy is the Lord Almighty; the whole earth is full of his glory' (Isaiah 6:3).

Compare this with the average run-of-the-mill church, even today's evangelical church, where there seems to be a great love of everything but this. What passes for worship in many churches today is anything and everything but what reflects the holy mind and nature of God or even pleases God. Worship in many cases is stiff and artificial, with no semblance of life in it. I am afraid many have truly forgotten what it means to worship God in the sacred assembly. There is ritual and routine aplenty but a lack of the overwhelming passion of being in the holy presence of God.

Some say the answer to all our problems in the church today is revival, as though that is a panacea for all our spiritual ills and shortcomings. Most people's idea of revival, however, runs the gamut of a week of meetings to a high-energy display of emotionalism. What is real revival? The kind that has changed the course of human history. Throughout church history, every revival has led to a sudden intensification of the presence of God, resulting in the spontaneous worship of God. Anything less is superficial, artificial and even detrimental to true spiritual health.

When the Holy Spirit came on the Day of Pentecost, why did the believers break out into ecstatic language? Simply, it was because they were rightly worshiping God for the first time. Intensive worship unexpectedly leaped out of their hearts. It was nothing planned or perpetrated by some 'worship leader.' God was in their midst. Whenever there is a move of the Holy Spirit, it is always a call for God's people to be worshipers of the Most High God above everything else. Whatever else revival does, it must restore the purpose and meaning of being a worshiper.

In the world created by God, nothing exists without meaning and purpose. Science seeks to discover the meaning of things and their relationship to one another, their interaction and effect upon one another. That is science. I have nothing against science; however, science and scientists deal only with short-term affairs, never with the overarching purpose of people's being created in the image of God.

Admittedly, science has made great strides in eliminating some diseases that in a former generation took the lives of thousands. And, for this, we all stand with heads bowed in utter profuse thanks. I grant you that science, especially medical science, has made great improvements in the quality of our life. But even that has limitations. Science can save a baby from diphtheria, save a teenager from smallpox, save a person in their twenties from polio, save a man in his fifties from a heart attack and keep him going right on until he is ninety in good health. But the question I posed is this: if he still does not know why he is here, what does he gain?

If he does not know why he is here and does not know his purpose, all you are doing is simply perpetuating the life without direction or purpose. If a person is living just because it is the best alternative to dying, what good is it?

Somebody observed about Christopher Columbus: 'Columbus went out not knowing where he was going and when he got there he did not know where he was and when he got back he did not know where he had been. And he did it all on other people's money.'

This is the way of religion today. People do not know where they are, they do not know where they have been, they do not know why they are here, they do not know where they are going, and they do the whole thing on borrowed time, borrowed money and borrowed thinking, and then die. Science may be able to help keep you alive but it cannot help you here. Science can keep you alive so you have longer to think it over, but it will never give you any answer for the purpose of your life.

When I was seventeen years old, I associated with a certain group of people. They were not educated people and certainly not scientists. They were plain, simple Christians, the saints and mystics, and the brethren of the common life. They were the people of God, and had a simpler and more beautiful view of the world than many scientists. They did not know much, certainly not as much as a scientist, but they did know why they were here and where they were going. They celebrated their purpose of life by worshiping God enthusiastically and unashamedly.

Suppose I were to visit some university and encounter a celebrated doctor of philosophy. I would not know nearly as much as he would know. However, if I met him downtown wandering around and he did not know where he was, I would know more than he would on that one thing.

He might stop me and ask, in a very cultured matter, 'Where am I?'

I could say to him, 'You're between Hamilton and Vineland.'

'Thank you,' he would say. I would smile to myself and think, I have not studied in Germany and I do not have all his degrees, but I know more than he did about one thing. I knew where he was and he did not.

I have read Albert Einstein's work on the fourth dimension and have never been able to understand it. I quit trying, but I take pleasure in knowing something Einstein did not know. I know why I am here. I belong to that company of plain Christians who believe a book called the Bible that says, 'In the beginning God created the heavens and the earth' (Genesis 1:1).

God made humankind in his own image and blew into them the breath of life to live in his presence and worship him. God then sent humankind out into the world to increase, multiply, and fill the earth with men and women who would worship God in the beauty of holiness. That is our supreme purpose.

I do not walk around with my head down, looking sad, because somebody has written more books than I have or knows more than I know or has been to school for longer than I have, because I have a little secret. I can tell you why I was born, why I am here and my everlasting duties while the ages roll.

The plain people I admire so much say God created the flowers to bloom so that humankind might enjoy them. God created the birds to sing for our pleasure. However, no scientist would be caught dead admitting something that simple. The scientist has to come up with some complicated reasons for what this all means. His problem is, he never begins with God.

The scientist would object and say, 'God did not create the birds to sing. Only the male bird sings and he sings only to attract a female so he can have a nest of little ones. That is just simply a biological fact, that is all.'

I think to myself, why couldn't the bird just warble or something? Why does the bird have to sing like a harp? Why do these birds sing so beautifully? Because the God who made them is the composer of the cosmos. He made them, put a harp in their little throats, surrounded it with feathers and said, 'Now, go sing.' And they have been singing ever since, much to my delight.

I believe God made the trees to bear fruit, but the scientist shrugs his shoulders and objects, 'There you go again, you Christians. What a hopeless bunch you are. The trees bear fruit not for you but so there are seeds so there will be more fruit.'

God made the fruit, blessed it and told us to help

ourselves. God also made the beasts of the field to clothe humankind and the sheep to give us wool so we can make a nice sweater to keep us warm in the winter. God made the humble little Japanese silkworms in the mulberry trees in order that we might spin their cocoons and make silk.

Throughout the Bible, the prophets and apostles all testify that God made us for a purpose and, according to them, that purpose is to sing his praises before the hushed audience of all creation. God created the silkworm to make silk, the bird was created to sing, the sheep for their wool. Everything in God's creation has its purpose.

Looking at the man he created, God said, 'I am making man in my image and man is to be above all other creatures.' Man's supreme purpose is to be above the beasts of the earth and the birds of the air and the fish of the sea, and even above the angels in the heavens. Ultimately, this man is to enter God's presence and unashamedly worship God, looking upon his face while the ages roll. That is why man was created; that is man's chief end.

Apart from that, we have no more idea why we are here. God gave you a harp and placed it in your own heart. God made you in order that you might stand up and charm the rest of the universe as you sing praises to the Lord Jesus Christ. That is why we were made in his image.

With the great hymn-writer Isaac Watts (1674–1748), we can sing:

'I'll praise my Maker while I've breath;
And when my voice is lost in death,
Praise shall employ my nobler powers:
My days of praise shall ne'er be past,
While life, and thought, and being last,
Or immortality endures.'

Prayer:

Lord God, for years we have wandered in the state of spiritual amnesia not knowing who we are, where we came from or what our purpose in life is. We did not know that we were made in your image for the single purpose of worshiping and adoring you. Our plight has been to lead an empty and futile life. Then Christ, through the work of the Holy Spirit, awakened us to our true purpose in life. Now our days are filled with praise. And we praise you with our whole being, honoring you and adoring you in the beauty of your holiness. Amen.

CHAPTER 2

Searching for Lost Human Identity

Christian ministry is based on the assumption that there are some serious-minded people who want to know who they are, what they are, why they are here and where they are going. Maybe not many compared to the great masses of the world's population, but enough to form a nice congregation almost everywhere you go. If I am wrong about this, I might as well leave my Bible closed.

But I firmly believe there are some who are serious and want to know the answer to the question, 'What is my purpose in life?' Unfortunately, the masses have been given the wrong answer, leading them farther away from the knowledge of God. This includes all the religions and philosophies of our world. This has been a neat and successful trick on the part of the enemy of human souls.

Many people have tried to answer that question and consequently led many other people astray. Let me take several of their answers now and point out how empty and futile they really are, and may God deliver us from such utter foolishness.

Work

Some would insist that our chief purpose in life is to work. No other place in the world from the days of Adam to this present time has given more honor to work than the North American continent. Not that we like to work; we just like to talk about what an honorable thing it is.

Have you ever stopped to consider what work is?

Let me put it in its simplest form. Work is moving things and rearranging them. We have something over here and we work to put it over there. Something is in the pail and we put it on the side of the house, which we call painting. Something is in the cupboard; we work to put that into a skillet and then on the table to put it into our family, and that is called cooking.

Smile at this simplification if you like, but you will find this definition of work a very good and sound one. Work is taking something that is somewhere, putting it somewhere else, and rearranging it. To the observer of humanity the obvious thing about work is the fact that it has a short-range focus; it never has a long-range purpose.

The farmer has some corn in his barn, puts it in the field and covers it up. After nature has worked on it for three or four months he takes it from there and puts it back where he got it, only there is more of it. The next year the corn is gone; the cattle ate the corn. Therefore, work always has a short-range purpose.

But what is the result of all this? Why do all this? Why put that green, red or white paint in that pail and put it on your house? You say, in order that it might not be affected by the weather, that it might stay nice and look nice.

That is very good, but there never was a house built yet that will not rot and get run-down and finally be replaced with something newer. Nobody can convince me I am merely made to work like a farm horse without having any future or any reason except that work. A man can work all his life, be identified by that work and then retire. Shortly after retirement, he dies because he has lost his purpose in life. The end result of work is utter futility.

Education

Somebody else insists we are here for a higher purpose than mere work. Our purpose is to educate ourselves, develop ourselves and perfect our intellectual nature. The process of this cultivation of the human mind is extensive.

A young person will go through school and be taught all the important things of life. She then might continue through college and learn science, art, literature and history. If she is ambitious, she will go on to do postgraduate work and get a degree.

I see only one little catch in this scenario. That young woman, educated and well cultivated, is going to die and take all that education with her to the grave. All that culture, that love of Bach, of Brahms and everything else will go right down with her into the grave.

Everything we do for a person is going to go right

down into the grave with them when they die. If they gain forty degrees, we can put that on their tombstone, but they do not know anything about it. They are dead. Education alone is not the reason we were born. Our purpose is not for the perfecting of our intellectual nature, and the education or development of our mind. I am not against education because the alternative is simple ignorance. Education, however, does not provide the eternal purpose for which I am here.

Pleasure

Others have a simpler viewpoint and tell us we are here merely to enjoy ourselves. Epicurus, the father of Epicureanism, taught that pleasure is the chief end of man. Unfortunately, he earned a terrible reputation, but his idea was not as bad as it sounds. Epicurus did not teach that our purpose was to go out on a three-week drinking binge or take drugs or engage in every physical and carnal pleasure known to man. He taught something quite the contrary.

He taught that pleasure is the end of all things: the pleasures of friendship and the beauty of literature and poetry and music and art. 'The noble pleasures of a good conscience', he said, 'is what we were born for in order that we might enjoy life.'

Although he had good intentions and tried taking the high road, he had it all wrong. Joys and pleasures all pass away.

An old man who used to sit and listen enraptured to the music of the classics now sits and nods in the corner and does not know Brahms from Frank Sinatra, because his mind is gone and his ability to enjoy pleasures is gone as well. What does a man do when life offers him no more pleasure? Some have answered this emptiness by suicide, a tragic end to a life that never found the real purpose of existence.

Thrills

The younger and more energetic among us have the idea that the thrills of life are all that matter. Experiencing all the thrills of life is the ultimate point of living. It is a philosophy, and is widely practiced and held by a good number of people who are not Christians. It is the philosophy that sex, food, sports, excitement, and the gathering of goods is the chief end of humanity and our purpose in life. Our purpose in life is whatever produces a thrill.

Those who dedicate their time and the purpose of their life to getting a thrill out of life are going to have one of two things happen to them. Either they are going to run down physically, or they are going to run down mentally until they lose all ability to experience any thrill any more.

Nothing is quite as pathetic as an old rogue who has no thrill left any more. A bored, weary, defeated, burnt-out old man who has spent his life seeking physical thrills wherever he could find them and at any cost, and now he is old, tired and worn out. Nothing thrills him any more. Trying to get through to him is like sticking an ice pick into a wooden leg. There is no response, no reaction, no life or feeling left.

If that is all life is for, I think God made a terrible mistake when he created this whole world. If that is all, then with my hand over my face I cry to God Almighty, complain, and say, 'Why did you make me like this?'

But the exciting news is that that is not the reason or purpose for our life. I bring you to the Scriptures themselves, not man's philosophy but what God says about our purpose in life. Scripture teaches us a number of things about the purpose of our life. It teaches us that God created all things out of his own pleasure. 'You are worthy, our Lord and God, to receive glory and honour and power, for you created all things, and by your will they were created and have their being' (Revelation 4:11).

When God decided to create humankind, it was a high day in heaven, accompanied by a big celebration – 'while the morning stars sang together and all the angels shouted for joy' (Job 38:7). Here was the heavenly host celebrating when God decided to create the heavens and the earth and in particular people to worship him.

This is taught throughout the entire Bible, that God created human beings to worship him. We are the darlings of the universe, the centerpieces of God's affection; however, many unbelievers denied this.

A very intelligent man once commented, when asked what he thought to be the biggest mistake or error made by people: 'I consider the biggest mistake to be the belief that we are special objects of Almighty God and that we are more than other things in the world and God has a special fondness for people.'

Regardless of that man's opinion, I base my whole life on the belief that God created people with a special, unique, divine purpose. I do not care how brilliant this man is; he cannot shake me from my conviction. It would be as useless as throwing cooked peas at a ten-story building to destroy any of my beliefs or doctrines or commitment to this faith.

When a little baby is born into the world, the father searches intently to see if the baby looks like him. He may be too tough to say it, but every father looks earnestly into that little wrinkled face to see whether it looks like him or not. We want things to look like us and, if they are not born to us, we go out and make them. We paint pictures; we write music; we do something because we want to create. Everything we create is a reflection of our personality. In the world of art a Monet is easily distinguished from a Rembrandt. Each painting reflects the personality of the artist.

God made humans to be like him so they could give more pleasure to God than all the other creatures. Only in human beings, as created by God, can God admire himself. We are the mirror image into which God looks to see himself. We are the reflection of the glory of God, which was the purpose and intention of God originally. Our supreme function through all eternity is to reflect God's highest glory and that God might look into the mirror called humans and see his own glory shining there. Through us, God could reflect his glory to all creation.

You are a mirror of the Almighty and this is the reason you were created in the first place. This is your purpose. You are not created that you might merely take something from over here and put it over there... *work*. You were not created only so that you might develop your brain so that you can speak with a cultured accent... *education*. Neither are we here to enjoy ourselves, even the pure pleasures of life... *pleasure*. Nor are we here for the thrills that life brings... *thrills*.

All the holy prophets and apostles teach that humans fell from their first estate and destroyed the glory of God, and the mirror was broken. God could no longer look at sinful people and see his glory reflected. We failed to fulfill the created purpose of worship of our Creator in the beauty of holiness. We forgot this, forfeited it by sin and are now busy finding other things to fill that emptiness. It is terrible what people will look to if they lose God. If there is no God in their eyes then they get something else in their eyes, and if they do not enjoy worshiping the great God Almighty who made them, they find something else to worship.

If a person does not have God, they have to have something else. Maybe it is boats, or maybe money, amounting to idolatry, or going to parties or just simply raising the devil. They have lost God and they do not know what to do, so they find something to do, which is why all the pleasures in life have been invented.

God made humankind to reflect his glory but,

unfortunately, we do not. The flowers are still as beautiful as God meant them to be. The sun still shines down from the spacious firmament on high. Evening shadows fall and the moon takes up the wonders and tells us whether the hand that made us is divine. Bees still gather their honey from flower to flower, and the birds sing a thousand songs, and the Seraphim still chant 'Holy, holy, holy' before the throne of God. Yet humans alone sulk in their caves. Human beings made more like God than any creature have become less like God than any creature.

Humanity, made to be a mirror to reflect the deity, now reflect only its own sinfulness. Sulking in their caves while the silent stars tell their story, human beings, except for their swearing, boasting, threatening, cursing and all the nervous and ill-conceived laughter and songs without joy, are silent before the universe.

Change the image now from a mirror to a harp. God has put in human beings a harp bigger than anything else, and he meant that harp to be tuned to himself. However, when people sinned and fell in this tragic and terrible thing we call the fall of man, they threw that harp down into the mud; it is full of silt and sand and its strings are broken.

The mightiest disaster ever known in the world was when the human soul, more like God than anything, more fitted to God's sweet music than all other creatures, let the light go from its mind and the love go from its heart, and began to stumble through a dark world to find itself a grave. From God's point of view humanity needed to be redeemed. What is the purpose of redemption?

Redemption is to restore us back to God again, to restring that harp, to purge it, cleanse it and refurbish it by the grace of God and the blood of the Lamb.

I have wonderful news for you. God who made us like that did not give up on us. He did not say to the angels, 'Write them off and block them from my memory.' Rather, he said, 'I still want that mirror to shine in which I can look and see my glory. I still want to be admired in my people; I still want a people to enjoy me and to love me forever.' Out of this insatiable passion, God sent his only-begotten Son and he became incarnate in the form of a man and, when he walked the earth, he was the reflected glory of God. God, finally, had his man.

The New Testament says, 'The Son is the radiance of God's glory and the exact representation of his being...' (Hebrews 1:3). When God looked at Mary's son, he saw himself reflected. Jesus said, 'Believe me when I say that I am in the Father and the Father is in me; or at least believe on the evidence of the miracles themselves' (John 14:11).

What did Jesus mean by 'When you see me, you see the Father's glory reflected'? 'I have brought you glory on earth by completing the work you gave me to do,' said Jesus (John 17:4), and there God glorified himself in his Son and that Son went out to die and all that glory was marred more than any man and his features more than the son of man. They pulled out his beard, bruised his face, tore out his hair and made lumps on his forehead. Then they nailed him on that cross where for six hours he sweated, twisted and groaned before finally giving up the ghost. The bells rang in heaven because humankind had been redeemed now. On the third day, he arose from the dead and now he is at God's right hand and God now is busy redeeming the people back to him again, back to the original purpose, to be mirrors reflecting God's glory.

I hope to explain what worship is and point out how tragically low this worship is among the churches. I hope to define worship and explain how we can recapture this worship for our generation and the generations to come.

Worship is humanity's full reason for existence. Worship is why we are born and why we are born again. Worship is the reason for our Genesis in the first place and our re-Genesis that we call regeneration. Worship is why there is the church, the assembly of the redeemed, in the first place. Every Christian church in every country across the world in every generation exists to worship God first, not second. Not tacking worship at the end of our service as an afterthought, but rather to worship God primarily with everything else coming in second at best. Worshiping God is our first call.

John Keats wrote of a tongueless nightingale (in *The Eve of St Agnes*): 'As though a tongueless nightingale should swell her throat in vain, and die, heart-stifled, in her dell.' Quite a figure of speech, really. I have often thought that this great figure of speech was a beautiful thing. The tongueless nightingale died of suffocation because it had so much song in it that it could not get it out. We are the other way around. We have such a tremendous tongue and such little use for it. We have a harp such as no other creature in God's universe but we play it so infrequently and so poorly.

When the saintly Brother Lawrence (c.1614–1691) was dying, somebody asked him what he was doing.

Without hesitation Brother Lawrence simply said, 'I'm just doing what I've been doing for forty years and I expect to be doing throughout eternity.'

'What's that?' they inquired.

'Worshiping God.'

As far as Brother Lawrence was concerned, dying was secondary; just an item on his agenda. His real occupation was worshipping God above and before all other things. He had been worshipping God for forty years, and facing death did not change that. When he felt his thoughts getting low, he was still worshiping God. He died and they buried his body somewhere, but Brother Lawrence is still worshiping God in that coveted place we call the presence of God.

You will be worshiping God long after everything else has ceased to exist. It is too bad if you do not learn to worship him now so that you do not have to cram for the last examination. For my part, I want to worship God in my own private life so fully and satisfyingly to the end that I will not have to cram for the final exam. I can nearly stop breathing with quietness and say, 'I worship him, I am still worshipping him and I expect to worship him for all eternity.'

That is what you are here for, to glorify God and enjoy him thoroughly and forever, telling the universe how great God is.

The Way of Perfection
(Frederick William Faber, 1814–1863)

Oh how the thought of God attracts
And draws the heart from earth,
And sickens it of passing shows
And dissipating mirth!

'Tis not enough to save our souls,
To shun th'eternal fires;
The thought of God will rouse the heart
To more sublime desires.

God only is the creature's home,
Though rough and strait the road;
Yet nothing less can satisfy
The love that longs for God.

Prayer:
O God of the universe, the God who created all things that exist, and created them for your pleasure, I humbly acknowledge you as my Creator. Restore to me the joy of your salvation. Restore the harp within that has been broken. Restring that harp in order that I might sing your praises throughout the universe and to all the angels populating your heavens. In Jesus' name. Amen.

CHAPTER 3

Discovering the Heart of Human Nature

To the diligent student, the Bible is amazing in its consistency. The whole import and substance of the Bible is unswerving in what it teaches: that God created humankind to worship him. That God, who does not need anything and who is complete in himself, nevertheless desires worshipers. God in his uncreated nature is self-sufficient and possesses no lack whatsoever, yet looks to people created in his image for worship. This represents a spiritual oxymoron. The Creator needs the creature.

This is the truth on which I want to build: that God made everything for a purpose. His supreme purpose in making people was to have somebody capable of properly and sufficiently worshiping him and satisfying his own heart. Humanity fell by sin and now is failing to carry out that created purpose. We are like clouds without water; they give no rain. Like a sun that gives no heat or a star that gives no light or a tree that no longer yields fruit, a bird that no longer sings or a harp that is silent and no longer gives out music.

This is the longing of God's heart; deep calling unto deep. The Bible insists that when our Lord will come he shall be admired; he shall be glorified first in the saints and admired in all that believe. There is glorification and admiration and our Lord is coming for that: '… on the day he comes to be glorified in his holy people and to be marveled at among all those who have believed. This includes you, because you believed our testimony to you' (2 Thessalonians 1:10).

The devil would like to tell us for our own unbelieving minds that God does not particularly desire our worship, as we owe it to him. Satan would have us believe God is not concerned or interested in our worship. But the truth is quite the contrary. God wants us to worship him and only redeemed people can worship him acceptably. We are not unwanted children, but God greatly desires our fellowship.

Why else would it be when Adam sinned and broke his fellowship with God that God came in the cool of the day and when he could not find Adam called out, 'Adam, where are you?' It was God seeking worship from Adam who had sinned and in rebellion broke his fellowship. The harp within Adam had become unstrung and the voice of Adam choked in his throat.

God has commanded us to worship him, and if you look at Psalm 45:11, 'The king is enthralled by your beauty,' God finds something in us that he put there for his personal pleasure. That 'beauty' belongs to God.

This is quite contrary to what is usually heard in the average evangelical pulpit. Not only does God want humanity to worship him but humanity, even in its fallen state, has something inside trying to respond but not succeeding. Usually, we are told that people do not want to worship God. However, there is not a tribe in the world that does not practice some kind of religion and form of worship. The apostle Paul talked about the whole world stretching out its hands as if by chance they might feel after God, so people *do* desire to worship God.

Isaac Watts expressed this for us in marvelous language in the hymn 'Eternal Power':

Eternal Power, whose high abode
Becomes the grandeur of a God,
Infinite lengths beyond the bounds
Where stars resolve their little rounds!

The lowest step around Thy seat,
Rises too high for Gabriel's feet;
In vain the favored angel tries
To reach Thine height with wond'ring eyes.

There while the first archangel sings,
He hides his face behind his wings,
And ranks of shining thrones around
Fall worshiping, and spread the ground.

Lord, what shall earth and ashes do?
We would adore our Maker too;
From sin and dust to Thee we cry,
The Great, the Holy, and the High.

Earth from afar has heard Thy fame,
And worms have learned to lisp Thy Name;

But, O! the glories of Thy mind
Leave all our soaring thoughts behind.

God is in Heaven, and men below;
Be short our tunes, our words be few;
A solemn reverence checks our songs,
And praise sits silent on our tongues.

When a man falls to his knees and stretches his hands heavenward, he is doing the most natural thing in the world. Something deep within compels him to seek someone or something outside of himself to worship and adore. In our unredeemed condition, human beings have lost our way and cannot clearly define the object of our wistful adoration, and so our search takes us far from God. When we do not find God, we will fill the void in our heart with anything we can find. That which is not God can never satiate the heart exclusively created for God's presence.

There is another facet of faith for our consideration. That is, we do not believe we are as dear to God as he says we are. We do not believe we are as precious or that he desires us as much as he does. The enemy of human souls has sold this lie to us, not only to beat us down, but to keep us from loving fellowship in God's presence. He cares not a bit for us, but his hatred of God drives him to do all in his power to deny God that which rightfully belongs to him. If everybody could suddenly have a baptism of pure cheerful belief that God wants and desires us to worship, admire and praise him, it could transform us overnight into the most radiantly happy people in the world. We would finally discover our purpose: to respond to the fact that God delights in us and longs for our fellowship.

If humanity had not fallen, worship would continue to be the most natural thing because God specifically designed us to worship him. God created people as his special instruments of music, offering to him natural sweet praise. However, when humanity rebelled and fell away from this purpose, when sin came into our life, sin became natural. Human nature is fallen, but this was not God's original intention for us. If everybody had cancer then we could say cancer was natural and accept it as such. However, it is not natural, because when God made the human body he did not have in mind wild cells forming themselves into tumours and destroying people.

When God made the human soul in his own image, he did it so that we might act according to that divine nature. He never intended the virus of sin to infect that sacred place within us. Sin, therefore, is the unnatural thing. It is a foreign substance defiling human hearts and lives, repelling God's gaze. Because of this condition in humanity, sin is natural and worship is unnatural, and so few people really do it.

Because of this, it is important to understand that nobody can devise their own pattern of worship or worship God in any way they please. The pleasure here belongs to God alone. The one who created us to worship him has also decreed *how* we shall worship him.

We cannot worship God any way we wish; our worship must always conform to God's pleasure. God does not accept just any kind of worship. He accepts worship only when it is pure and when it flows from a heart under the inspiration of the Holy Spirit. Only this type of worship, compatible with his holy nature, can possibly be accepted by him.

The suggestion that we should just worship God in any way we want and on our own whim and all will be well, as long as we are sincere, is a deception that destroys the lives of a multitude of people in every generation. It is a favorite ploy of the devil and a favorite pet view of unconverted poets.

The fallacy here is the fact that religious experience itself is actually quite possible apart from Christ and apart from redemption. It is entirely feasible to have an authentic religious experience and not be a Christian, and be on your way to an eternal hell. It happens all the time all over the world.

It might be hard to understand but it is entirely possible to have an experience with God and yet not have a saving experience with God. So not only is it possible to have a religious experience apart from Christ and apart from salvation, but it is possible to have worship apart from Christ and apart from salvation. It is chilling to think that it is possible to go through the motions of worship and not worship right. 'They worshiped they know not what,' said Jesus of a certain group. It is possible to have elements of worship: adoration, self-abasement and surrender, and yet still not be redeemed at all.

Thomas Carlyle (1795–1881), in his lecture 'On Heroes, Hero-Worship and the Heroic in History', warned us not to make the mistake of thinking that the great pagan religions of the world were all counterfeit. He said, 'It's not true they were phony; they were real and the terror of them was that they were real.'

I once visited an old church in Mexico that had an earth floor. I walked in and took off my hat and observed all the statues and candles. While there, I saw an old Mexican woman come in and walk straight down to the front as if she knew the way and could go in the dark with her eyes closed, because she had been there so often. She walked straight to a statue, I think it was of the Virgin, knelt and looked up into the face of that statue with a longing and devotion that I would like to see turned to the Lord himself. She was having an experience of worship and it was real to her. She was no phony; she was a real worshiper, but look what she was worshiping. Her worship was not aimed in the right direction. The sad part about this whole thing is that she did not know it.

The American Indian would stand on the bank of the river, stretch his arms up to the sky and say to the Manito, 'Praises be, praises be to the Manito, praises be.' He was experiencing real worship when he cried to his Great Manito.

It is entirely possible to have a religious experience without God and even while rejecting the God of the Bible. It is possible to have an experience of worship but not according to the will of God and, consequently, totally unacceptable to God because God hates idolatry.

Idolatry is simply worship directed in any direction but towards God, which is the epitome of blasphemy.

The apostle Paul understood this: '… the sacrifices of pagans are offered to demons, not to God, and I do not want you to be participants with demons. You cannot drink the cup of the Lord and the cup of demons too: you cannot have a part in both the Lord's table and the table of demons' (1 Corinthians 10:20–21).

Our Lord said that there would be a day when people would say, 'Lord, Lord, did we not prophesy in your name, and in your name drive out demons and perform many miracles? Then I will tell them plainly, "I never knew you. Away from me, you evildoers!"' (Matthew 7:22–23). He did not accept their worship. He *could* not accept their worship because it was not in accordance with the holy nature of God. God cannot accept any worship that is apart from himself and incompatible with his holiness.

The one who made us to worship him has also decreed how we should go about worshiping him. We cannot worship God as we like, according to our pleasure or mood. God does not accept just any kind of worship. He accepts worship only when it is pure and directed by the Holy Spirit. God has rejected almost all the worship of humanity in our present condition. However, God wants us to worship him, commands us to and asks us to. Obviously, he was anxious and hurt when Adam failed to worship him. Yet, nevertheless, God condemns and rejects almost all the worship of humanity.

Worshipers must submit to God's truth or they cannot

worship God. They can write poems and have elevated thoughts when they see a sunrise. But they cannot worship God except in faith and according to God's revealed truth. To worship in a way that God can accept means submitting to the truth about God, admitting who God says he is and admitting that Christ is who and what he says he is.

Furthermore, worshipers have to admit the truth that they are as sinful as God says they are. This is the last barrier to repentance. Humanity in its lost condition refuses to own up to its sinfulness. 'God made me this way,' we boast, to alleviate any personal guilt. If I am not responsible for my condition, I do not need to make any changes. God has to accept me as I am.

Then we have to admit to the truth of the atonement, the blood of Jesus Christ that cleanses and delivers us from sin, and come God's way. When people finally own up to their sinful condition, they are often tempted to try to make their own atonement. But this has a major flaw. It does not meet God's standard.

For our worship to be acceptable to God, we must be renewed after the image of him who created us. That 'image' must be restored. Only the renewed person can worship God in a way worthy of and acceptable to him.

If the Holy Spirit does not help us do these things, our worship would be only wood, hay and stubble. My worship will never reach higher than the top of my own head and God in heaven will refuse it as he refused the worship of Cain. I have a book, the Bible, which enlightens me. Here is the 'light that lights every man' who will read it. Jesus Christ is the 'light that lights every man who comes into the world'. The light of the human heart and the light of this book harmonize and, when the eyes of the soul look to the living Word of God, then we know the truth and we can worship God with truth and in spirit.

In the Old Testament, a priest could not offer a sacrifice until he had been anointed with oil, symbolic of the Spirit of God. No one can worship out of their own heart. Let them search among the flowers; let them search among the birds' nests and tombs and wherever they choose to worship God. Such a search will be futile and will lead to spiritual frustration.

A person cannot worship out of their own heart. Only the Holy Spirit can worship God acceptably, and he must in us reflect back to God his own glory. If it does not reach our hearts, there is no reflecting back and no worship.

How big and broad and comprehensive and wonderful the work of Christ is. That is why I cannot have too much sympathy for the kind of Christianity that makes out that the gospel is to save a person from smoking or drinking. Is that all Christianity does, keep me from some bad habit, so I will not bet on the horses, beat my wife, or lie to my mother-in-law? Of course, regeneration will clean that up and the new birth will make a person right. Those are the effects of a nature redeemed by the blood of Christ.

The primary purpose of God in redemption is to restore us to the divine imperative of worship so we can hear God say again, 'The king is enthralled by your beauty' (Psalm 45:11). 'Honor him, for he is your Lord.'

The church militant conquered the world with their joyous religion because and only because they were worshipers. When the Christian church in any generation ceases to be a company of worshipers, their religion succumbs to mere outer effects, empty works and meaningless rituals.

When you begin to talk about the Lamb who was slain and the blood that was shed and God the Father, God the Son and God the Holy Spirit, then you are living and worshiping in truth. When the Spirit of God takes over we worship in spirit and in truth, and that worship exceeds mere external rituals.

God created us to worship him, and when fundamentalism lost its power to worship, it invented religious claptrap to make itself happy. That is why I have hated it, preached against it, and condemned it all these years. While claiming to serve the Lord, the only joy such people have is a joy that is of the flesh. Elvis Presley was a happier man after he got through with his sensuous music than many Christians are after they have worked themselves up in an emotional frenzy for half an hour.

For the redeemed, the well of the Holy Spirit is an effervescing artesian well and we do not have to prime the pump. The silver waters of the Holy Spirit flooding up and out of the redeemed and cleansed heart of a worshiping person are as sweet and beautiful to God as the loveliest diamond. We need to learn how to worship to please the God who deserved it.

'The king is enthralled by your beauty; honour him for he is your Lord.'

Prayer:

God our Father, we seek you in ways that will bring us to you. We turn to the Holy Spirit to be our guide and teacher. May our hearts yield to his work and may he so flood our hearts with unspeakable joy and make us so full of glory that we rise above the din of the world into the light unapproachable. Amen.

CHAPTER 4

Paths in the Wrong Direction

Although the most natural thing for a man or woman to do is worship, and there is something within compelling them towards worship, not all paths lead to the worship God accepts and delights in. There are certain kinds of worship that are abhorrent to God and which he cannot accept, even though they are directed toward him and meant to be given to him. The God who desires worship insists that the worship be on his terms, and allows no exception.

Let me name them for you. These four categories are evident in every generation and culture, having withstood the passing of time.

Cain's worship

Cain's worship is beautiful in many respects and represents human efforts at their best. It is giving God what we delight in, disregarding God's command. God has condemned and rejected the worship of Cain, because it is worship lacking atonement.

Abel offered to God the sacrifice of blood while his brother Cain offered sacrifice without blood.

Cain approached God without a blood sacrifice, which is atonement; Cain came to God with a gift of his choosing for his Creator. He plucked a nice bunch of flowers and some delicious fruit and took it to God. God inquired after the blood and Cain said, 'What blood?' Cain did not understand that he could not come to God without blood atonement. And Cain objected, 'I don't care about sin, I'll just bring a gift.' He came before God with a bloodless sacrifice and offered flowers and fruit and the growth of the earth to the Lord.

This false worship of Cain was based on three errors.

First of all, Cain's worship rested upon a mistaken assumption regarding the nature of God. Cain was born of Adam and Eve, fallen parents, and had never heard the voice of God in the garden himself. When Cain came to worship God, he came to a God of his own imagination.

Abel, on the other hand, brought a lamb, and God accepted it. Quite naturally, God refused Cain's worship, which made him so mad he went out and in a jealous rage killed his brother. Cain did not comprehend the difference God saw between the two offerings. He took it upon himself to assume what would please God completely, disregarding the nature of God.

Cain's type of worship is all around us even today, even within the confines of what is called the Christian church. A man can be well educated and even graduate from a seminary and be taught how to use his hands and how to open his mouth and sound learned. He can be a ready-made preacher with all the culture the world of religion can offer. But, if he follows Cain's form of worship, no matter how beautiful it might be, it will not be acceptable in God's eyes.

Worship that is acceptable to God is based on knowing the nature of God. Cain did not know the kind of God he was, and therefore thought that sin was nothing to God – a gross misunderstanding of God's nature.

The second error of Cain's worship was that human beings have a relationship to God that they do not in fact have. Cain assumed he belonged to God and that he could talk to God without an intermediary. Cain failed to understand that he was alienated from God by his sin. Nothing in Cain's worship dealt with this sin element that separated him from God. He acted as though there were no such separation and ignored the implications of such a separation.

Many religious people mistakenly assume that humans have a relationship to God that they do not have. They think and teach that we are all God's children and we talk about the God and Father of humankind. The Bible does not teach that God is the Father of humankind, in fact it teaches the exact opposite. To assume a relationship that does not exist prohibits a person from really knowing God.

The third error of Cain's worship was in the area of sin. Cain assumed that sin was less serious than God viewed it. Consequently, Sin is dismissed as inconsequential to our worship of God. Sin, however, is serious and God never smiles upon it and never looks at any heart with sin upon it. He hates sin because sin has filled the world with pain and sorrow but more importantly, sin has robbed man of his purpose in life of worshiping God.

Cain thought God was a different kind of God from what he is. He thought he was a different kind of man than what he was and he thought sin was less vicious and serious than God said it was, so he came cheerfully bringing his sacrifice and offered God worship, which is simply worship without atonement.

While God says, 'He is your Lord, worship him,' and while he calls 'Where are you?' and while he commands that we must worship him in spirit and in truth, he bluntly and severely rejects worship not founded on redeeming blood.

I would not spend one hour in any church that did not teach blood atonement by the cross that did not teach redemption by the blood of Jesus Christ the Lord. I would not spend one minute where they did not teach it because Cain worship, no matter how gentle and tender it is and how it may be adorned with beautiful flowers plucked from all parts of the world, it is still false and God frowns upon it because it is false in itself. God simply rejects Cain worship.

Pagan worship

If Cain worship is man at his best, then pagan worship is man at his worst. Completely disregarding all dignity, people subject themselves to the basest elements of their nature, worshiping the creation instead of the Creator. I would need to write a five-foot-long shelf of books, if I were able to do it, to set out adequately the tenets of this. I could go back if I wanted to and research the worship of the early Egyptians, the Egyptian book of the dead and the writings of Zoroaster and Buddha. We could make a case and talk about the worship of the pagans, or heathen worship.

Paul talks about this and does not have a kind thing to say about it. He condemns it outright and downright and says, 'For although they knew God, they neither glorified him as God, nor gave thanks to him, but their thinking became futile and their foolish hearts were darkened' (Romans 1:21). And down they went from God to man and from man to bird from bird to beast and from beast to fish and from fish to creeping things that wiggled on the earth. That was humankind's terrible trip downward in their worship.

This is humanity trying its best to be its worst, and succeeding. God rejects and completely disowns this kind of worship and any worshipers involved in it.

Why do I include this in this book of worship?

It is my opinion that if the Christian church has not crossed the line already, it is perilously close to slipping into pagan worship, rendering to the creature what rightfully belongs to the Creator.

Let me explain what I mean. Never has there been a time in Christian history when the church has been more plagued with celebrities than today, especially in the music department.

On a Saturday night, a 'praise and worship band' will

hold a concert in the concert hall downtown. After one song the audience explodes into applause accompanied by cheers and a standing ovation. To cover his tracks, the lead singer will say, 'Let's give a clap offering to God.'

If you do not think this is getting near to crossing the line, do this. Take the lyrics of the song that caused such uproar and give it to one of the dear old saints at church on Sunday. Make sure it is one of those saints with an impeccable reputation for holiness and unimpeachable Christian character. Usually this will be one of the saintly prayer warriors of the church. Have this person take these lyrics to the pulpit and read them quietly to the audience. If it does not create the same effect as the night before, maybe it was not the truth in those lyrics that the people the night before were applauding but the performance.

Pagan worship always mirrors the culture around it rather than the Christ within.

Samaritan worship

Then there is Samaritan worship, which is heretical worship in the correct meaning of the term. A heretic is not a man who denies all the truth; he is just a very fastidious man who picks out what he likes, rejecting what he does not like or what does not suit him at the time. Certain aspects of theology appeal to him but others are rejected because those do not suit him at the time. I refer to these as inconvenient aspects of theology.

I heard of a man addressing a large group of Christian young people and offering to them this advice: 'Don't believe anything in the Bible that doesn't square with your own experience.' This man had the infinite effrontery to tell young people searching for truth to take the word of God and judge it by their wicked little hearts. How can you get any worse than that? That is Samaritanism. That is heresy. Heresy means I take what I like and I reject what I do not like. The very word 'heretic' means one who picks and chooses.

But the Bible says, 'And if anyone takes words away from this book of prophecy, God will take away from him his share in the tree of life and in the holy city, which are described in this book' (Revelation 22:19).

The Samaritans were heretics in the right sense of the word because heretical does not always mean false. A person can be a heretic and not teach anything particularly false. A heretic is not necessarily one who teaches that there is no Trinity, that God did not create the earth or that there is no judgment. Heresy does not necessarily mean teaching wrong. It is the selecting and rejecting aspects of truth, and applying psychology, humanism and various religions of all sorts. Every religion is based on this.

The Lord rejects Samaritan worship because of this selective nature. It picks what it likes and what does not inconvenience its lifestyle. If it does not like something, it explains it away and goes on as if it were a small matter or even did not exist.

The Samaritans were heretics in that they chose

certain parts of their Bible, the Old Testament. They had a Pentateuch and accepted that, but rejected certain parts of David, Isaiah, Jeremiah, Ezekiel and Daniel, 1 and 2 Kings, the Song of Solomon and other parts of the Scripture. They believed them and did some translating. You can translate anything and prove anything you want to prove. All a person has to say is, 'I know Greek', or 'I know Hebrew', and after that, they are on their own. They are self-appointed experts on the subject.

Every false religion or cult is built on the selecting of favorite Scripture passages to the neglect of other passages. They do not compare scripture with scripture, which opens the door for heretical doctrine to come in.

The Samaritans translated the old Pentateuch in such a way that Samaria became the place of worship. And of course, they were hostile to the Jews, who insisted Jerusalem was the only place to worship Jehovah. The Samaritans used their translation of the Pentateuch to prove their position.

God gave Israel Moriah and here on this hill, David established the city of Zion and Solomon built the temple and that was the place where people should worship. It was there Christ came and became the sacrificial Lamb for the sins of mankind.

However, the Samaritans refused Jerusalem in favor of Samaria and did so by selecting certain parts of the Pentateuch that supported that position.

I do not think I will have to spell it out and mark it in red ink for you to see how much heresy there is these days: believing what we want to believe; emphasizing what we want to emphasize and following along in one path while rejecting another. Doing one thing but refusing another. We become heretics by picking and choosing among the words of God that suit us at any given time. That is Samaritan worship.

Nature worship

I admit I have more sympathy with this category than I do with liberalism. At the same time, I reject nature worship, which is but the poetry of religion. Religion does have a lot of poetry in it; it is proper, and it should have. Personally, I melt like honey on a hot day when I get to this nature worship business because it is the poetry of religion. Poetry is the high enjoyment and contemplation of the sublime.

By nature, we are all poets, and religion brings poetry out more than any other occupation the mind can be engaged in. Moreover, there is a lot that is very beautiful about religion. You will discover a high enjoyment in the contemplation of the divine and sublime. And the concentration of the mind upon beauty always brings a high sense of enjoyment.

Some mistake this nature worship, this rapt feeling, for true worship. It is an understandable mistake.

God warned Israel that, when they got into the Promised Land, looked up and saw the sun and the stars, they were not to get on their knees and worship them because Jehovah would destroy them from out of the land.

The world is full of these worshipers of God through nature, which is a better way to say it. It is a high enjoyment, a concentrating of the mind upon beauty as distinct from the eye and the ear. If your ear hears beauty that is music; if your eye sees beauty that is art, but if you think beautiful thoughts without music or art then that is poetry. We write what we feel inside, and that is poetry.

Some people understandably mistake such rapturous feelings for worship. Ralph Waldo Emerson said, 'I have crossed the meadow after a rain on a moonlight night when the moon had come out and the rain and the puddles were still lying in the meadow and the moon shining on the little puddles of water in the grass and I have been glad to the point of fear.' He was so happy he was afraid. I have felt it myself. Emerson did not believe in the deity of Christ and the blood of Christ and resigned from his church rather than serve Communion. He eventually denied the faith. Yet he was glad to the point of fear because he was a good man. He was a great man, a poet and an artist. A mighty man indeed, but I do not think God accepted his worship at all because it was nature worship.

Also, it is easy to confuse the music of religion with true worship because music elevates the mind and raises the heart to near rapture. Music can lift our feelings to a sense of ecstasy. Music has a purifying effect on us to the extent that it is possible to fall into a happy and elevated state of mind with only a vague notion about God, and imagine that we are worshiping God when we are doing nothing of the sort. We are simply enjoying an ecstatic moment that God put in us, which even sin has not yet been able to kill.

I reject the idea of any poetry in hell; I cannot believe that among the terrible sewage of the moral world there is going to be anybody breaking into similes and metaphors and I cannot conceive of anyone breaking into song in that terrible place called hell. We read about music and poetry in heaven because it belongs there. As far as I know my Bible, we never hear about it in hell. We hear about conversation in hell but we do not hear about song because there is no song there. There is no poetry there, there is no music there, but there is plenty of it on earth – even among the unsaved, because they too were made in the image of God. While they have lost God from their mind, they still appreciate the sublime and carry within their innermost part a residue of spiritual desire.

Certain people have written books on the importance of sublimity and how to cultivate it. And there is much that is sublime and beautiful in the world. Regarding beauty, sublimity is beauty of the mind in contradistinction (to use a long word) to beauty of the eye and ear. Music is the beauty that the ear recognizes. And certain other beautiful things the eye recognizes, but when the heart hears nothing and sees nothing but merely feels, then it is the music of the heart. It is beauty within the spirit.

The Scripture tells us that 'God is spirit, and his worshipers must worship in spirit and in truth' (John 4:24). The word must clear away all the mists of obscurity. It takes worship out of the hands of people and puts it in the hands of the Holy Spirit.

Therefore, we can have all that and still not worship God at all or even be accepted by him.

I repeat that we can be nature worshipers, pagan worshipers, Samaritan worshipers and Cain worshipers, and God Almighty sternly rejects it all and says, 'I will have nothing to do with it.' Jesus our Lord said, 'God is spirit, and his worshipers must...' I want you to see that word, that imperative, there: 'God is spirit, and his worshipers *must*...' the word 'must' clears away all mists of obscurity and takes worship out of the hands of mere human beings.

It is impossible to worship God acceptably apart from the Holy Spirit. The operation of the Spirit of God within us enables us to worship God acceptably through that person we call Jesus Christ, who is himself God. Therefore, worship originates with God, comes back to us and is reflected from us; that is the worship God accepts, and he accepts no other kind.

Prayer:
O God, we ask you that, as we speak, heaven might be open and there might be a sense of your presence and the feeling that there is impending upon this world another world above, an eternal world touching you. As the kingdom of heaven touches the kingdom of earth, we believe that God has heard our prayers. O God, we pray that you would speak and not let us take anything for granted; let us not believe that something is true when it is not true, or assume we are all right when we are not or think that our worship is acceptable when it is not.

May we, one and all, each and every one of us, come humbly looking to the sacrifice, the mighty sacrifice, and hear the words of love and see the mighty sacrifice and have peace with you. Grant this, we pray, in Christ's holy name. Amen.

> *Still, still, without ceasing,*
> *I feel it increasing,*
> *This fervor of holy desire;*
> *And often exclaim,*
> *Let me die in the flame*
> *Of a love that can never expire!*

**The Fervor of Holy Desire
(Jeanne-Marie Bouvier de la Motte Guyon,
1648–1717, translated by William Cowper)**

CHAPTER 5

Religion versus Worship

John 4:24

Since the expulsion from the garden of Eden, religion has been an intolerable burden on the back of all humankind. In spite of the drudgery, it is a bondage most are unable or unwilling to break. The word 'religion' itself means 'to bind back', and religious people, as a rule, have laid off one set of chains only to take up another. Whatever it takes, humanity will exercise this inward impulse to worship.

Then along comes our Lord and issues a long-awaited spiritual emancipation proclamation and signs it in blood. Now the people of the world, bearing the heavy yoke of religion, can know the true freedom of genuine worship. Our Lord Jesus spoke words allowing the light to shine upon us so that there is light in our spirits, elevating us and lifting us up out of the mud of depraved society.

God never called us to walk knee-deep in the sludge of the world, nor did he intend for us to be mired down in human traditions. Therefore, the Lord sets us free and opens a fountain of healing water for the wounds of the world.

In spite of all this, we deliberately choose the bondage of religion over the liberating freedom of Christ.

In India, they believe that the goddess Ganga, that is,

the Ganges River, has power to cleanse people. Certain saints make pilgrimages to bathe in goddess Ganga, one of the dirtiest rivers in the world. They will fall down full-length and then mark with their finger where their forehead was, step forward and put their foot where the mark is and then fall full-length again. Literally, they fall across scores of miles to the goddess Ganga, the River Ganges, and bathe themselves, go away and are no cleaner than they were before. In fact, they are not even as clean as they were before. Certainly, they are wounded and sorely bruised in their soul.

Our Lord puts into one sentence the words of worship: 'God is spirit, and his worshipers must worship in spirit and in truth', forever settling this matter and emphasizing that we cannot please God by bruising our body, or by bathing in this or that river. Instead, we must worship the Father in spirit and in truth. This is the true healing water for the wounded souls of religious people.

Our Lord explains here that worship is natural to human beings. There has never been a tribe of people discovered anywhere that did not have religion as part of their society. It was perfectly natural for Adam to walk with God in the garden in the cool of the day. The years of Adam were blessed by the velvet-soft healing voice of God. When Adam sinned, he hid from the presence of God among the trees of the garden. He was conscious of God but he was not free to worship God because sin had come in between and torn the strings off the harp. Nothing remained but the outline; the music of the soul was muted; now there was cacophony and discord where once there had been harmony. So he lost the proper object of his worship and was now looking about for something else to worship. We worship by the necessity of our being. Looking around for something to worship, we recognize mystery and wonder. The result is that whatever we cannot explain, we will worship. Whatever evokes wonder becomes the object of our worship. Because the human mind is fallen, we are amazed at external things and objects that impress.

The human mind is enlarged, lifted and filled with wonder and this very wonder leads to worship and opens mystery to us. People used to stand on the seashore and hear the moaning of the sea and watch the gulls turn and see the white clouds float and they would cry, 'What is all of this, what is all of this?' And they called that something out there Neptune and said, 'This is our God,' and they got on their knees and made sacrifices to Neptune. The splendor of nature called to mind a need to worship not the Creator but the creation. When they saw the sun rising in the morning and making its journey across the sky and setting in the sea of blood, they said, 'What is this shining thing that always rises in the same place and goes down and never fails?' They called it Phoebus Apollo. Apollo was a great and beautiful god – they made him out to be a god with silver wings on his feet because he went so fast across the sky. They worshiped and said this is wonderful. They did not know what it was, but it was wonderful and inspired a need to worship. The Parsis got on their knees before the sun; they called it 'Mazda', and the light that shines down is

Mazda light named after the god of the Zoroastrians, the fire worshipers.

If we do not know how to worship through Jesus Christ, our Lord, the human heart will break out somehow like a flood that pours over the riverbanks and it will worship. If it does not get going in the right direction, it will go in the wrong direction but it will worship.

Not only in nature did humanity find reason to worship, but also within their own heart and emotions. They said, 'Look at love, look at this powerful, tremendous thing for which men and women die and think nothing of it. Look at this that binds a man and woman together, binding family together, binding men to the love of their country until they will give and sacrifice themselves freely.' They called it Venus; we have named one of the planets after that goddess. We could go on: there is Ceres, the goddess of life, and many others; the list is as endless as the human imagination. Every emotion, every thought, every imagination of humankind became the object of mystery and adoration all leading away from the one behind all this, the Creator.

Another indication of this need to worship can be seen in the artistic and creative work of human beings. What makes someone want to create something beautiful? Why do they want to write a poem, paint a picture, compose a piece of music? I believe fallen people have within them somewhere in the deep of their soul something that calls out after mystery. Deep calls unto deep at the noise of God's waterspout; the deep voice of God calls, and the deep of humanity struggles to answer back.

Every time a Greek got onto his knees at the seashore and offered his sacrifice to Neptune, it was the little blind deep within him answering back to the deep of God. Every time an American Indian stood on the shore of the river and reverently put the bones of the fish back into the sea and apologized to God for killing it and eating it, and every time he looked up and said, 'Manito', and 'Praises be', he was giving up to the mystery within him. And every time that great genius, Beethoven, turned out a page of immortal music he was feeling something deep within. He said, 'I know God; he is nearer to me than he is to others; I know this God,' and then he wrote his imperishable music. What was he doing? Flinging out wildly, looking to worship something, anything. This great man who hovered back and forth between suicide and life until he gave up and went the way of all flesh was only an example.

It is an innate characteristic of human beings to do this, to admire and to fear, and many religions have developed because of this. In India there is a god for everybody, to cater for the internal compulsion to worship. By nature, we have to admire something. Within our very being we have to adore, and if we lose this ability to adore in our spirit and soar in our heart we will find some other way to do it. We will get out there somehow. Because of how we were created, human beings are drawn to mystery wherever they find it. We need some mystery that creates within us a sense of awe, and when we find it we will worship.

This is the impulse behind exploring other worlds and riding out into the vast spaces in the heavens. None

81

other of God's creatures does it, and no other creature thinks of doing it. Human beings, who have lost the mystery of God within their hearts, look for that mystery elsewhere.

The woman in John chapter 4 revealed what is wrong with the entire religious world. 'Sir, I understand from what you say that you are a prophet. You know more than the average person would know; you must be a prophet. I've got a question for you.' This question was not simply a frivolous one; it was one that separated Jew from Samaritan even though they were related by blood. The question was, 'Here in Samaria, on our holy mountain, we worship. Across there a little way in Jerusalem, on the holy mountain of the Jews, they worship. And we say this is the place to worship and you say Jerusalem is the place to worship. Now you are a prophet: tell me where is the right place to worship.'

This woman falls into her own little trap and reveals that chief woe of the religious world: do I worship here or do I worship there? Do I worship in this church or do I worship in that church? Which church is the right church and what denomination is the right one? That is the difficulty and the problem. The whole problem then was externality of worship. Externalism is our problem even today, the biggest problem the church faces.

Jesus our Lord said this beautiful thing: '... a time is coming when you will worship the Father neither on this mountain nor in Jerusalem. ... a time is coming and has now come when the true worshipers will worship the Father in spirit and truth, for they are the kind of worshipers the Father seeks.' If God were a local deity confined to a hill, you would have to go to the hill to worship him. If God were a river deity confined to the river, you would have to go down to the bank of the river to worship him. If God were a mountain deity or if God were a plains deity, you would have to go wherever he was. Jesus gave us the marvelous liberating news that God is spirit; therefore God is everywhere, and we do not worship in places any more.

The purpose of nature is to lead us to the Creator so we can worship him. The purpose of human feelings and emotions is to lead to the one who implanted those within our hearts, the Creator. Everything in all of creation is to point to the Creator and evoke adoring wonder and admiration and worship. Wherever we go, we can worship.

Jesus taught essentially that we are portable sanctuaries and, if we are worshipping in spirit and in truth, we can take our sanctuary around with us. Jesus said, 'Don't you see that if God is spirit, worship is spiritual and anything spiritual has no location in space and it has no location in time.' You do not get up in the morning, look at your calendar and say 'This is the time to worship.' You do not get up, go out, look around and say 'This is the place to worship.' You worship God now, anywhere, any place, any time, because worship is spiritual.

People have made a comedy of religion, because they have enslaved themselves to externals and objects to the point of the ridiculous. These religious pilgrims travel to their holy shrines in order to worship. Many will make a pilgrimage to the Holy Land and believe they are closer to

God there than anywhere else on the planet. In God's kingdom, as he has intended it, no place is holier than another. If you cannot worship here, you cannot worship there.

It does not stop here, this bondage of religion. Some make their religion consist in foods. Some things they do not eat and some things they eat. The result is that if they do eat it, they are holy, and if they do not eat it, they are not holy, and vice versa. At certain times of the year you can eat this but not at other times of the year. Paul explained that what you ate did not make you better and it did not make you any worse. It might make you sick but it will not make you holy, and it will not hurt you nor help you. If it is decent and good and you can digest it, help yourself. Holiness does not reside in the food we eat and worship is not dependent on that food either. God is spirit and they that worship him must worship him in spirit and in truth.

Then some are enslaved to times. Worship is not limited to times. I respect our brethren who follow the church calendar year, which begins with one thing and ends with another, but I do not follow it at all. Can you imagine that for six weeks out of the year I repent, then after that the lid is off? I could not imagine myself being tied down to times. 'Behold, now is the accepted time.' This is the time, so any time is all right. You can say, 'Good morning, God,' in the morning. You can say, 'Goodnight, God,' at night. You can wake in the night and think of God; you can even dream of God – I have. You can have God any time, any place.

There are of course times of the year when we think of

religion a little more. I personally like Easter. If I were to have a time of the year it would be Easter, because that is when birds are returning from Florida and the people of God are looking up and we are hearing, 'Christ the Lord is risen today, hallelujah, hallelujah.' I like Easter and I think it is a beautiful time of the year. I have a tough time preaching Easter sermons because all of my sermons are based upon his resurrection and if you take away the resurrection of Jesus Christ my sermons collapse.

Christ's resurrection is not truer at Easter than at any other time of the year. Without the resurrection of Christ, all of Christianity falls to the ground. Our worship cannot be confined to time.

Foods are not holy, times are not holy and places are not holy. If they do not point to Christ, they become a snare enslaving us to mere religious bondage.

The Jews made the mistake of thinking the Temple was holy, and because the Temple was holy nothing could happen to the Temple. Jesus pointed out their error. 'See this Temple? See these stones? Every bit of it will lie in the dust before very long.' It came down to the ground in the year AD 70. He said Israel is like a tree. 'See that ax, either the tree will bear fruit or it will be cast down into the fire.'

I am talking about worship now and saying worship is a spiritual thing. It is internal, and external things are unnecessary. Now, for instance, we could not sit on the street corner and preach, sing and pray. We need walls to protect us or heat to keep us warm. Buildings have a place and purpose, so I am not against buildings. You have to have books and I am for books. God has blessed external things but the trouble is we become slaves to them instead of making them our servants.

So it is with times and foods and everything else: they are our servants. Therefore, we rise above all the little things of religion and look down on them from our place in the heavenlies. It is wonderful how little things look when you are up high enough. You always know you are losing altitude when things begin to get big. When fields get to be the size of postage stamps you are up there. When they begin to get a little bit bigger, you are losing altitude; you look at your watch and say, 'We're going to land.' The further down you get into the world the bigger things look, and the higher up, the smaller. I recommend to you, concerning that the big problem facing you, that you rise above it, take off and get up there above it.

True worship elevates us above all the accoutrements of religion into that rarified atmosphere of God's holy and delightful presence.

Madame Guyon put these thoughts into a hymn we often sing in church:

My Lord, how full of sweet content,
I pass my years of banishment!
Where'er I dwell, I dwell with Thee,
In heav'n, in earth, or on the sea;
Where'er I dwell, I dwell with Thee,
In heav'n, in earth, or on the sea.

Prayer:

We praise you, O God, that our religion lies not in what we do or eat or where we go. You have set us free from all externals so that we can elevate ourselves above all these and find your heart and worship you. Amen.

Chapter 6

Seekers after Truth

In this mixed-up world in which we live there is a group of people claiming to be seekers after truth. 'We are seekers after truth,' they boast, as if that qualifies them as acceptable worshipers, no matter what their beliefs might be or the truth they are seeking. Some churches actually accommodate this idea and invite people to 'come to our church, you do not have to believe anything, just be a seeker after truth.' This infers a certain openness of mind accepting anything and everything. In this frame of mind, truth is not absolute but whatever you think of it at the time, or, whatever you determine to be truth.

On the surface, these 'seekers after truth' seem to be genuine in their belief or at least heading in the right direction. However, in this day of relativism, truth means different things to different people. What is true for one person may not necessarily be true for another. And what was true yesterday may not be true today. The only thing these 'seekers after truth' accomplish is keeping people from seeking the absolute truth, which is Jesus Christ, '… the same yesterday, and today and forever.'

Then there are those who inform us that there is truth in every religion. This is like saying that there is water in most poisons and so it is all right to drink. It is not the water that kills, it is the poison. The more ambiguous the poison, the more dangerous it is. The closer it is to the real thing, the more damage it does. And the enemy of human souls knows this all too well.

When you study the religions of the world you will find much in them that is true. However, partial truth is actually more dangerous than trickery. When I know something is an outright lie I can stay away from it.

Going back to the garden of Eden, we see this. The serpent did not lie to Eve outright. He simply told her partial truth. He told her only what he wanted to tell her in order to mislead her to his advantage. It is what he did not tell her that created all the problems following the fall in the garden.

You can tell someone something and not actually lie to him or her but so present the truth that it keeps him or her from the truth.

I can go down to the local zoo and look at a tiger. There it is lying before me licking itself like a big kitten. Perhaps it is in a playful mood and I can say to myself that this tiger is not dangerous. Why, it is just a big kitty. The tiger can be de-clawed and all those dangerous teeth extracted. But the partial truth does not change the nature of the tiger. By nature, it is the most efficient killing machine on God's green earth. Its playfulness is only partial truth. Now, if I approach that tiger only accepting partial truth, I am putting myself in mortal danger. It is what you do not know that can hurt you.

These who boast that they are seekers after truth are putting themselves, and others, at greater risk than I would face in the tiger's cage. The tiger can harm only the body, but these partial religious truths can effectively lead me into everlasting spiritual darkness and final damnation.

Every false religion in the world has a basis of truth about it. It starts with some truth and then moves away from it subtly and maliciously. Maybe not intentionally. Eve did not intentionally disobey God or knowingly move away from ultimate truth.

When it comes to the worship of God, we must be quite careful that we are not basing it on partial truth, but on the entire revealed truth such as can be found in the Bible.

People want to worship God, but they want to worship God the way *they* want to worship God, according to their own comprehension of truth. So did Cain, so did the Samaritans and so have we down the years, but God has rejected it all. Now there is an imperative to worship deep within the heart of humankind, but with God there is no tolerance, there is no broad spirit. There is the sharp pinpointing of fact so that every person in their own fallacy is completely rejected.

I have piles of religious poetry and I have read most of it. People who have not found God and have not experienced the new birth and who do not have the Holy Spirit in them still have the ancient impulse to worship something. If they come from a developing country where there is still little education they might kill a chicken, put feathers on their head and dance around a fire, calling for a witch doctor. However, if they have some education, they write poetry.

Edwin Markham was an American poet who wrote two or three good things. He wrote 'Lincoln', and 'The Man with the Hoe', and that is good poetry. However, I quote him because this is an example of the way the human mind works. The world is full of bushel baskets of poetry like this that you can throw out. The kind of poetry and religion that has no anchor, no God, no high priest, no blood, no altar, but floats around like a drunken butterfly, floating and flopping about not knowing quite where he wants to go, and they all say about the same thing:

I made a pilgrimage to find the God;
I listened for His voice at holy tombs,
Searched for the prints of His immortal feet
In the dust of broken altars; yet turned back
With empty heart. But on the homeward road
A great light came upon me and I heard
The God's voice ringing in a nesting lark;
Felt His sweet wonder in a growing rose;
Received His blessing from a wayside well;
Looked on His beauty in a lover's face;
Saw His bright hand send signal from the sun.

He was a good poet in many respects but his ornithology was not very sound. In the first place, nesting larks do not sing. In the second place, he said he heard God singing like a bird. Then he said, 'I felt his sweet wonder in a swaying rose and received his blessing from a wayside well. Looked on his beauty in a lover's face. Saw His bright hand send signals from the sun.'

Now there you have it: not a crazy man and not a medicine man from the jungles of New Guinea. Here is a man whose poetry is in every anthology. He writes as one of the poets of the world and he goes out looking for God. And he searches for him in the first place in a graveyard, and does not find him. He looks at broken altars and cannot find him there, and then on the way back he hears a bird singing and says that is God. And he sees a happy lover holding hands with his girlfriend and says that's God. And he sees a rose waving in the wind and he says that's God. So he comes home and writes himself a poem.

Now, I want to know, how could he get this bad? That this man, in a land of Bibles, with the gospel being preached, writes that he went looking for God in altars and tombs and in all dark dusty places and didn't find him and started for home and saw him and heard him singing in a nesting lark, saw him in a rose and saw him in the face of a young lover. Then he looked up and, lo and behold, God was signaling from the sun. I never had any signals from the sun myself and I do not know of anybody except Edwin Markham who wrote about such a thing.

This kind of thing, it seems to me, needs to be exposed. We need to tell the world that God is spirit and those who worship him must worship him in spirit and in truth. It must be the Holy Spirit and truth. You cannot worship him in spirit alone, for the Spirit without truth is helpless. It cannot be in truth alone, for that would be theology without fire. It must be the truth of God and the Spirit of God. When a person yielding to and believing the truth of God is full of the Spirit of God then their warmest and smallest whisper will be worship. So we can find we will worship God by any means if we are full of the Spirit and yielded to the truth. However, when we are neither yielded to the truth nor full of the Spirit there is no worship at all. God cannot receive into his holy heart just any kind of worship.

Jesus said, 'Those who worship him must worship in spirit and in truth,' and settled forever how we should worship God. God formed the living flame and he gave the reasoning mind that only he may claim the worship of humankind. So that instead of our worshiping God, everyone worships in their own fashion.

Keep in mind that there is only one way to worship God. 'I am the way and the truth and the life. No one comes to the Father except through me' (John 14:6). Instead of being kindly and charitable by allowing an idea to stand that God accepts worship from anybody anywhere, I am actually injuring and jeopardizing the future of the person I allow to get away with that. Anything incompatible with the holy nature of God only damages a person's soul and ultimately damns that soul forever.

I would do as Isaac Watts did when he tried to put the Psalms in meter. He just could not leave a psalm alone if there was nothing about Jesus in it. He would always put a stanza in there before he would be done with it. Personally, I am glad he did.

It is an either/or situation. Either a worshiper must

submit to God's truth or he or she cannot worship God at all. People can write poems and they can get elevations of thought when they see a sunrise. They can hear the fledgling lark sing but a fledgling lark does not sing. And they can do all sorts of things but they cannot worship God except in faith. To do so would mean they have to surrender to the revealed truth about God. They have to confess that God is who he says he is and what he says he is. And they have to declare that Christ is who he says he is and what he says he is. They have to own up to the truth about themselves and admit that they are as bad sinners as God says they are. Then they must acknowledge the truth of the atonement, the blood of Jesus Christ that cleanses and delivers from that sin. Finally, they have to come God's way. They must be renewed after the image of him that created them.

Only the renewed person can worship God acceptably. Only the renewed person can embrace the truth as God has revealed it in his word.

So these people who have churches and pray in the name of the all-good and almighty Father have no idea of what true worship, acceptable in the eyes of God, is and stumble in spiritual darkness. I would rather go out in the park and walk with my New Testament. I can find my God – not the god in a rose, but the God who sits on the throne on high and by his side sits the one whose name is Jesus. Having all power in heaven and on earth. And I could commune with God walking out on the street rather than worship him at an altar of Baal.

Humankind must be renewed. We must have had an

infusion of the spirit of truth. Without an infusion of the Holy Spirit, there can be no true worship.

How big God is and comprehensive the work of Christ; how imperative is repentance and regeneration in the Holy Spirit. By rejecting the Holy Spirit, we put out our eyes and blunder on in darkness, sightless and lost. Let us not be guilty of that in this day of easily available Bibles and plenty of truth.

Bernard of Clairvaux (1091–1153), in his great hymn, expresses the heart of all those truly seeking after truth:

Jesus, Thou Joy of loving hearts,
Thou Fount of life, Thou Light of men,
From the best bliss that earth imparts,
We turn unfilled to Thee again.

Thy truth unchanged hath ever stood;
Thou savest those that on Thee call;
To them that seek Thee Thou art good,
To them that find Thee all in all.

We taste Thee, O Thou living Bread,
And long to feast upon Thee still;
We drink of Thee, the Fountainhead,
And thirst our souls from Thee to fill.

Our restless spirits yearn for Thee,
Wherever our changeful lot is cast;
Glad when Thy gracious smile we see,
Blessed when our faith can hold Thee fast.

O Jesus, ever with us stay,
Make all our moments calm and bright;
Chase the dark night of sin away,
Shed over the world Thy holy light.

Prayer:

O God, how wonderful is the work of your Son. It fills the whole universe with wonder and awe and admiration. My heart is overwhelmed with the intensity of that work within me. I seek you, but I find you only when I have sought you with my whole heart and mind. My wonder at you has all but exhausted my expressions of praise and worship. Your presence is my comfort day and night. Amen.

CHAPTER 7

What Came First: Workers or Worshipers?

'I believe in one God, the Father Almighty, maker of heaven and earth and of all things visible and invisible, and in one Lord Jesus Christ, the Son of the Father, begotten of him before all worlds. God of god and Light of light, very God of very God begotten not created.'

'Thou art the true glory, O Christ, thou art the everlasting Son of the Father.'

'When I took upon me to deliver man, Thou didst humble thyself to be born of a Virgin. When Thou hadst overcome sharpness of death Thou hast opened the Kingdom of heaven to all believers.'

These ancient assertions or creeds, as they are sometimes called, were made by the church down the centuries, declaring itself with great joy and a sense of deep unworthiness. I join my voice with theirs and say I believe these things and I believe that he, 'the king of glory, the everlasting Son of the Father, took it upon himself to deliver man and overcame the sharpness of death and by the resurrection has now opened the kingdom of heaven to all believers'.

In light of this, the human mind must give an answer to some questions. One of them is what is the reason for all this: 'God of gods and Light of light, he was born of the virgin, served under Pontius Pilate, overcame the sharpness of death and opened the kingdom of heaven to all believers'? Behind this must be a purpose, for God has intellect. Intellect is one of the attributes of deity and therefore God must have a reasonable purpose behind this that can stand up under the scrutiny of sanctified human reason. Why did God do all this?

As an evangelical, I am deeply worried and concerned to the point of some degree of suffering over the state of evangelicals these days. By evangelicals, I mean the free churches generally. The churches that have order, that do not have order and the ones that have disorder. The churches that have beautiful services and plain services, hit-and-miss and off-the-cuff services and churches whose ministers feel they must be a cross between St Paul, Moses and Bob Hope.

The supreme reason the Lord was born of the Virgin Mary to suffer under Pontius Pilate, to be crucified, die and be buried, the reason he overcame death and rose again from the grave, is that he might make worshipers out of rebels. We are the recipients of a grace meant to save us from self-centeredness and make worshipers out of us.

Thomas Boston said the difference between humans and beasts is that a beast looks down and a person is made to look up. A person can engage with the God above while the beast goes about and sees only the ground underneath its short legs. But people can see into the heavens above. A beast bows under its burden but people lift their hearts in praise to their burden-bearer, Jesus Christ.

God is infinitely more concerned that he has worshipers than workers.

Unfortunately, most evangelicals do not share this concern. For the most part, evangelicals have been reduced to the position where God is a supervisor desperately seeking for help. Standing at the wayside, he tries to see how many helpers will come to his rescue and bail him out of a tight spot. If we could only remember that, as far as his plans are concerned, God does not need us. We mistakenly believe that God needs workers and so we cheerfully say, 'I'll go to work for the Lord.'

I think we should work for the Lord, but it is a matter of grace on God's part. However, I do not think we should ever work until we learn to worship. A worshiper can work with eternal quality in his work but a worker who does not worship is only piling up wood, hay and stubble for the time when God sets the world on fire. God wants worshipers before he wants workers. He calls us back to that for which we were created, to worship the Lord God and to enjoy him forever, and then out of our deep worship flows our work for him. Our work is acceptable to God only if our worship is acceptable.

Many of the great hymns of the church came out of revival of some kind. They can be traced through the Lutheran Reformation, the Wesleyan Revival and the Moravian Revival. These hymns were born out of the times when the church of God labored. The Spirit fell upon it, heaven was opened, the church saw visions of

God, and radiance beaming from the throne above was reflected from the hearts of his people.

If the devil has a sense of humor, I think he must laugh and hold his sooty sides when he sees a church of dead Christians singing a hymn written by a spiritually awakened and worshiping composer. There are many great hymns that I didn't like in my early days because I heard them sung in some dead prayer meeting with a dead song leader who did not expect anything and a dead congregation in front of him who did not expect anything. Both would have been shocked if anything had happened. They had a spirit of non-expectation. True worship that is pleasing to God creates within the human heart a spirit of expectation and insatiable longing.

We must understand that the Holy Spirit descends only on a heart engaged in worship. Out of your fiery worship, God will call you to work for him. But he is not interested in you jumping up and starting some slapdash religious project. This is where the contemporary church is today. Any untrained, unprepared, spiritually empty rattletrap of a person who is a bit ambitious can start something religious: The Fig-Leaf Gospel Tabernacle. People listen to them and work to try to help this person who never heard from God in the first place. Many confuse this wild amateurism as spiritually dynamic worship and offer it to God. From my point of view, nobody who worships God is likely to do anything offbeat or out of place. Nobody who is a true worshiper indeed is likely to give him- or herself up to carnal and worldly religious projects.

Every glimpse we have of worshiping creatures or of heaven shows people worshiping. I read Ezekiel 1:1–28, and think about these strange beautiful creatures with wings, high and lifted up; creatures that put down their wings and dropped quietly by the throne of God in reverent worship. At the voice of the Lord, they raised their wings, went straight forward and did not turn as they went. I love that too. This is a glorious picture of the creatures and God's people worshiping in ecstatic wonder and adoration.

Then you find rapturous worship in the sixth chapter of Isaiah: 'In the year that King Uzziah died, I saw the Lord seated on a throne, high and exalted, and the train of his robe filled the temple. Above him were the seraphs, each with six wings. With two wings they covered their faces, with two they covered their feet, and with two they were flying. And they were calling to one another: "Holy, holy, holy is the Lord Almighty; the whole earth is full of his glory." At the sound of their voices the doorposts and thresholds shook and the temple was filled with smoke.' They were worshiping God in joyous and awesome wonder. Not with irreverent, emotional outbursts that serve only to stroke the flesh.

Worship is also found in the book of Revelation (4:9–11): 'Whenever the living creatures give glory, honor and thanks to him who sits on the throne and who lives for ever and ever, the twenty-four elders fall down before him who sits on the throne, and worship him who lives for ever and ever. They lay their crowns before the throne and say: "You are worthy, our Lord and God, to receive glory and honor and power, for you created all things and by your will they were created and have their being."'

A little further on: 'Then I heard every creature in heaven and on earth and under the earth and on the sea, and all that is in them, singing: "To him who sits on the throne and to the Lamb be praise and honor and glory and power for ever and ever!" And the four living creatures said, "Amen", and the elders fell down and worshiped' (Revelation 5:13–14)

I see a wonderful picture of some class of being called 'elders'. I do not know whether they are elders such as we elect in our churches, or not. Then there are beasts that are otherwise called living creatures. They are all worshiping the Lord God and, wherever you look in heaven, you will find them engaged in worship. If worship bores you, you are not ready for heaven. Worship is the very atmosphere of heaven focusing on the person of Jesus Christ.

I believe in justification by faith as strongly as Martin Luther ever did. I believe we are saved only by faith in the Son of God as Lord and Savior. But what concerns me is an automatic quality about being saved nowadays. It works something like this: simply put a nickel of faith in the slot, pull down a lever and take out the little coin of salvation, tuck it in your pocket and off you go. It is that simple. After that, you say you are saved. When questioned you simply say, 'I put the nickel in; I accepted Jesus and I signed the card.' Very good; there is nothing wrong with signing a card so we can know who they are. It is the only way we know some people are Christians. How tragic.

Christianity is not a result of coming to God and becoming an automatic cookie-cutter Christian, stamped out with a die: 'one-size-fits-all'. 'What God has done for others he'll do for you.' These are marvelous mottos with a grain of truth in them, but they lead just as far from the absolute truth. We come to Christ so that we might be individually redeemed and remade in the image of Christ – vibrant, personal Christians, loving God with all our heart and worshiping him in the beauty of holiness.

Not only is worship the normal employment for moral beings but worship is the moral imperative. The book of Luke (19:37) tells us, 'When he came near the place where the road goes down the Mount of Olives, the whole crowd of disciples began joyfully to praise God in loud voices for all the miracles they had seen.' Some believe they are worshiping when they are making a lot of noise and chatter and racket. They can never worship without noise and commotion. Religious noise and worship do not necessarily mean the same thing.

On the other hand, I want to warn you cultured, quiet, self-possessed, poised, sophisticated people so sure of yourselves that it embarrasses you if anybody says 'Amen' out loud in a church meeting: Throughout history, the people of God were always a little bit noisy.

I often think of that dear English mystic of 600 years ago, Lady Julian of Norwich. She was meditating on how high and lofty Jesus was and yet how he 'meeked' himself down to the lowest part of our human desire, and she just could not control herself. She let out a shout and prayed aloud in Latin, which translated into English meant, 'Well, glory to God. Isn't this a marvelous thing?'

If that bothers you, something is wrong.

Our Lord was faced with such criticism. When Luke writes that '… the whole crowd of disciples began joyfully to praise God in loud voices for all the miracles they had seen', I am quite sure they were not all in tune.

When you get a crowd of people whom the Lord has blessed and when they go out of themselves with worship and joy, they are just as likely as not to praise God a little bit off-key.

'"Blessed is the king who comes in the name of the Lord! Peace in heaven and glory in the highest!" Some of the Pharisees in the crowd said to Jesus, "Teacher, rebuke your disciples!"' (Luke 19:38–39). It offended the Pharisees to hear anybody singing glory to God out loud. So they said to Jesus, 'Master, rebuke your disciples.'

'"I tell you," he replied, "if they keep quiet, the stones will cry out"' (Luke 19:40). Jesus said in effect that he was to be worshiped. Those Pharisees would have died in their tracks if they had heard a rock praising the Lord. These poor people were praising God at the top of their voices.

Worship is a moral imperative and yet I believe it is the missing jewel in evangelical circles. The crown is here but the jewels are missing. The church has decked herself with every ornament but one shining gem is missing, the jewel of worship.

This thing has practical implications in the local church. For example, a man will never attend a prayer meeting but finds himself on the church board making decisions for the entire church. He would never go to a prayer meeting because he is not a worshiper; he is just a fellow who runs the church, and in his mind he can separate the two. My friends, you cannot separate the two.

I do not believe anyone has a right to debate a church issue or vote on it unless he or she is a praying, worshiping person. Only a worshiping person has the ability to make spiritual decisions within the context of the local church. If we are not worshipers, we are wasting other people's money and only piling up wood, hay and stubble to be burned at the last day. It might be business as usual but it is not glorious worship.

Worship is an awesome thing and I would rather worship God than do any other thing I know of in the entire world.

If you were to go to my study, you would discover piles of hymnbooks. As a singer, I leave a lot to be desired, but that is nobody's business. My singing is an expression of my worship of the Almighty God above. God listens while I sing to him old French hymns and translations of the old Latin hymns and old Greek hymns from the Eastern Church. And, of course, the beautiful songs done in meter as well as some of the simpler songs of Watts and Wesley and the rest. The Christian hymnal is a beautiful place to begin a daily regime of worshiping God.

Some might point out that it is a waste of time to spend

our time worshiping God. 'There is work to be done for the Lord,' we are told. There is no time for loafing about, as though worship was in the category of loafing. The beautiful part about this is that if you worship God, you will be an active person.

People ablaze with the radiant worship of God did every deed done in the church of Christ. The great mystics, the great hymn-writers and the great saints were the ones doing all the work. The saints, who wrote the great hymns we sing, were active to the point at which you wondered how they ever did it. George Whitefield, John and Charles Wesley, St Bernard, Tersteegen and other names you could roll off, wrote our hymns of faith. The more intense their worship, the more extensive their work. Hospitals grew out of the hearts of worshiping men. Asylums for the insane grew out of the heart of worshiping people. Worshiping men and women learned to be compassionate to those whose minds had failed them.

Look at some of the great advances in civilizations and you will discover that they were made by worshiping men and women. Whenever the church came out of its lethargy and rose from its spiritual slumber into a renaissance and revival, worshipers were always at the back of it all.

We are called to worship and we are failing God when we are not worshiping to the fullness of our redeemed potential. When we substitute worship with work we are failing God in ways we can hardly imagine. When the glory of God came down on the temple in olden days, the priest could not stand and minister, such was the awesome presence of God.

When a traveling salesman got to the town where Charles Finney's revival was going on in New England, he sensed something was happening. He asked the first man he met about it. Something was different, he could feel it.

He was told, 'There's a revival in this town, God is here and people are being converted, saloons are being closed up, half-way houses are being nailed shut. Men and women are cleaning up. Evil men are quitting their daily habits and getting right with God. God's in this place.'

This is what we lack in evangelical churches. We do not have it in our Bible conferences, in our camp meetings, or in our churches. Most churches today are run the way you would run a club or business, and it grieves my heart. I wish we could get back again to worship so that, when people entered church, they would find God's people worshiping and fall on their faces and say, 'Truly God is in this place of truth.'

The presence of the Lord is the most wonderful thing in the entire world. I once prayed under a tree with some preachers and a Salvation Army captain. I prayed and the others prayed. Then the Salvation Army man began to pray. I cannot remember a word he said but I knew that here was a man engaging God in an awesome, marvelous, elevated feeling in the holy act of worship.

As a lad, I belonged to a very liberal church. At the time, I did not know any better. One Sunday night a little girl got up to sing. She was a hunchback and had a face that looked as if she had suffered a lot. Her appearance did not generate much expectation, at least from me. However, when she began to sing, something changed. What a beautiful little face she had. She stood there and sang with a child's voice. She was worshiping God.

This is missing in our churches. We used to sing an old hymn written by Isaac Watts:

Bless, O my soul! the living God.
Call home thy thoughts that rove abroad.
Let all the powers within me join
In work and worship so divine,
In work and worship so divine.

Bless, O my soul! the God of grace.
His favors claim thy highest praise.
Why should the wonders He hath wrought
Be lost in silence and forgot,
Be lost in silence and forgot?

Why indeed should the wonders he has wrought be lost in silence and forgotten? Why should we be silent about the wonders of God? Let the whole earth confess his power; let the whole earth adore his grace. The Gentiles shall join with the Jews in worship and work so divine.

That is what a church is supposed to be, not a big ecclesiastical machine with someone turning the crank with a big smile you could not wipe off, who loves everybody and whom everybody loves. He has the building to pay for, and turns the crank and the machine runs.

110

This kind of thing seriously grieves my heart. I want to be among worshipers. I want to be among a people who know the presence of God in their midst, resulting in radiant and sometimes ecstatic worship.

Prayer:

Dear Lord Jesus, we love you and we love your holy Father. We love the blessed Holy Spirit, the Comforter, the Lord and giver of life, who with the Father and Son together is worshiped and glorified; we love you, O God. We expect to spend eternity with you, not standing behind worshiping at the altar, but like the creatures out of the fire worshiping with trembling joy and then rising to go and do your service somewhere in the far reaches of the creation and hurrying back to the throne to report, O God.

We look forward to this. We used to feel death is a terrible dark ugly cruel river but in another way it's a door into a new light and we love to look into your face and see your people, see Abraham and Isaac and Jacob, and sit down in the kingdom of God with your people and every tongue and tribe and nation around the world. O Lord, prepare us now for that hour. Teach us the protocol of heaven; teach us the etiquette of the kingdom. Teach us now so we will not be doing anything strange when we pick up our harp and join the company innumerable or sing in the choir invisible. Bless this people, Lord. Holy Spirit, shine with light divine upon this heart of mine. Holy Spirit, with power divine, come, we pray,

CHAPTER 8

The Components of True Worship

'The king is enthralled by your beauty; honor him, for he is your Lord' (Psalm 45:11).

Worship is not confined by emotion and feelings but is an inward attitude and a state of mind subject to degrees of perfection and intensity. It is not possible always to worship with the same degree of wonder and love as at other times, but it always has to be there.

A father may not always love his family with the same intensity when he is tired and his business is having trouble. Although he may not have a feeling of love towards his family at the time, it is there because it is not just a feeling. It is an attitude and state of mind and a sustained act subject to varying degrees of intensity and perfection.

This embodies a number of factors, both spiritual and emotional. With this in mind, I want to give you a definition of worship as it ought to be found in the church.

First, worship is to feel in the heart.

I use that word 'feel' boldly and without apology. I do not believe we are to be a feelingless people. I came into the kingdom of God the old-fashioned way. I believe

I know something of the emotional life that goes with being converted, so I believe in feeling. I do not think we should follow feeling but I believe that, if there is no feeling in our hearts, we are dead. If you woke up in the morning and suddenly had no feeling in your arm, you would call a doctor. You would dial with the left hand because your right hand was dead. Anything that has no feeling in it you can be quite sure is dead. Real worship, among other things, is a feeling in the heart.

Worship is to feel in the heart and express in some appropriate manner a humbling but delightful sense of admiring awe. Worship will humble a person as nothing else can. The egotistical, self-important person cannot worship God any more than the arrogant devil can worship God. There must be humility in the heart before there can be worship.

When the Holy Spirit comes and opens heaven until people stand astonished at what they see and in astonished wonderment confess his uncreated loveliness in the presence of that most ancient mystery, then you have worship. If it is not mysterious, there can be no worship; if I can understand God then I cannot worship God.

I will never get on my knees and say, 'Holy, holy, holy' to that which I can figure out. That which I can explain will never ever awe me, never fill me with astonishment, wonder or admiration. But in the presence of that most ancient mystery, that unspeakable majesty which the philosophers have called a 'mysterium tremendum,' which we who are God's children call 'our Father who is in heaven', I will bow in humble worship. This attitude ought to be present in every church today.

Blaise Pascal (1623–1662) was one of the greatest minds that ever lived. When he was only in his teens, he wrote advanced books on mathematics that astonished people. He became a great philosopher, mathematician and thinker.

One night he met God, and his whole world was changed. He wrote down his experience on a piece of paper while it was still fresh in his mind. According to his testimony, from 10.30 p.m. to about 12.30 a.m. he was overwhelmed by the presence of God. To express what he was experiencing he wrote one word: 'Fire.'

Pascal was neither a fanatic nor an ignorant farmer with hayseeds behind his ears. He was a great intellectual and thinker. God broke through all that and, for two solid hours, Pascal experienced something he could only characterize later as fire.

Following his experience he prayed, and to keep a reminder of that experience he wrote it out: 'O God of Abraham, God of Isaac, God of Jacob, not of the philosophers and the wise.' This was not a prayer for somebody who reads their prayers; this was not formal religious ritual. This was the ecstatic utterance of a man who had had two wonderful, awesome hours in the presence of his God. '… the God of Abraham, the God of Isaac, the God of Jacob, not the God of the philosophers and the wise. God of Jesus Christ, Thy God shall be my God, forget the foolishness of the world and God who can befriend only in the way taught in the gospel. O righteous Father, the world has not known Thee but I have known Thee, joy, joy, joy, tears of joy.' And he put an 'Amen' after that, folded it up, put it in his shirt pocket and kept it there.

That man could explain many mysteries in the world but was awestruck before the wonder of wonders, namely Jesus Christ. His worship flowed out of his encounter with that 'fire' and not out of his understanding of who and what God is.

I have given a running definition of worship, and now I want to break it down and define four major factors or ingredients in worship.

One is boundless confidence in the character of God.

Many cannot rightly worship these days because they do not have a high enough opinion of God. In our minds, God has been reduced, modified, edited, changed or amended until he does not resemble the God Isaiah saw high and lifted up but something else again. And, because he has been reduced in the minds of the people, we do not have that boundless confidence in his character that marked a former generation of Christians.

Confidence is necessary for respect. Without confidence in someone, it is difficult to respect them. Extend that upward to God. If we cannot respect him, it becomes impossible to worship him. In the church today, our worship rises and falls altogether depending on whether the idea of God is low or high. We must always begin with God, where everything begins. Everywhere and always God has to be antecedent, God is always there first, always previous, always prior. The God who is there is not the homemade cheap god you can buy these days marked down because he's shelf-worn. However, the

God and Father, the awesome God, the mysterious God, the God who watches over the world and holds the universe in his great hands, this God we must worship.

One thing needed in this time is a reformation of worship. Our concepts of God must be rescued from the deplorable depths to which they have sunk. God needs no rescue but we must rescue our concepts from their fallen and frightfully inadequate condition, which hinders pure and delightful worship.

Boundless confidence is one thing. Without absolute confidence in God, I cannot worship him. It is impossible to sit down with a person and have fellowship with them if you have reason to fear they are out to get you or are tricking or deceiving or cheating you. You have to respect them before you can sit down quietly and enjoy mutual fellowship, which is the core of pure worship.

When we go to God, we must raise our affections and our confidence to God. And in the presence of God we must be without doubt or nervousness or worry or fear that God will cheat us or deceive us or let us down or break his covenant or lie or do something wrong. We have to be convinced to the point at which we can go into the presence of God in absolute confidence and say, 'Let God be true though every man be a liar.' The God of the whole earth cannot do wrong, and when we can do this in the presence of God it is the beginning of worship.

The second component in our worship is admiration.

It is possible to respect a person and not especially admire them. The same would apply to God. Someone may have a theological respect for God that is purely academic. At the same time, they may not particularly admire what they see, or may even be unable to admire. But when God made us in his own image, he gave us a capability of appreciation, the ability to appreciate and admire our Creator.

One of the greatest Bible teachers of his generation, Dr David Watson, talked often about the love we have for God. He taught two kinds of love: the love stemming from gratitude and the love of excellence. We could love God because we were grateful to him or we could go on past that and love God because of what he was. It is possible for a child to love her father or mother out of gratitude, which is proper and right; she should of course do that. Years later, when she gets to know her parents or maybe after they are gone, she will remember she loved them also out of the love of excellence.

Some people we are supposed to love but there is no excellence there. We have to love them with infused love; we cannot love them with a love called out by their excellence. God Almighty is excellent, beyond all other beings. He is excellent and so this love of excellence surpasses the love stemming from gratitude. God's children rarely get beyond the love we have for him because he has been good to us. You rarely hear anybody in prayer admiring God and worshiping the excellence of God and talking to God about his own excellence. The Psalms do, Christ did and the apostles did, but we do not hear it much now. This generation has produced Christians who are primarily Santa Claus Christians, eagerly looking for God to put up a Christmas tree with all our gifts under it. We are grateful to God, and it is right and proper that we should be because of all the things he does for us and all the good that he gives us, large and small. That is, however, only the lower elementary kind of love.

Going beyond that we come to the love of excellence, where we can go into the presence of God and not want to rush out again but stay in the presence of God, because we are in the presence of utter infinite excellence. Naturally we admire this, and this knowledge can grow until our heart has been lifted into the excellence of love and admiration.

The third component I find in worship is fascination.

Fascination is to be full of moral excitement. You cannot read your Bible very long until you find that God fascinated some people. They were fascinated by him and were filled with a high moral excitement. It would be difficult to find much of this today in the average church in America.

Wherever God is truly known by the Holy Spirit's illumination, there is a fascination and a high moral excitement. A fascination captured, charmed and entranced by the presence and person of God. It is to be struck with astonished wonder at the inconceivable elevation and the magnitude and the splendor of God.

For me, it is either God or agnosticism. I do not know many churches I would want to join and get into the rat race. I do not want to be part of any religious group where each person is merely a cog in the wheel: the pastor turns the crank and, if it comes out all right at the end of the year and there is no deficit, he is a good man. I am not interested in that at all. I want to begin with God and end with God. Of course, I can never end with God because there is no end in him.

Many of the hymns of the church came out of this sense of admiration and fascination in the hearts of men.

'O Jesus, Jesus, dearest Lord! Forgive me if I say, for very love, Thy sacred name a thousand times a day.' That came from a man, Frederick W. Faber, fascinated by what he saw. He admired God until he was charmed and struck with wonder at the inconceivable elevation and magnitude and moral splendor of this being we call God.

The fourth component is adoration.

Adoration is white heat made incandescent with the fire of the Holy Spirit, and to love with all the powers within us. It is to feel, to love with fear, wonder, yearning and awe. I shudder when I think of how many are doing things today in regard to worship in the church completely counter to this spirit of adoration. Adoration cannot be conjured up by the manipulation of some worship leader.

Sure, they preach about Jesus dying for us and say, 'Now, if you believe that and accept him everything will be all right.' But there is no fascination, no admiration, no adoration, no love, no fear, no wonder, no yearning, no awe, no longing, no hunger and no thirst. I wonder if they really have met God at all. How could they and not be elevated into the holy atmosphere of adoration?

A young couple have their first baby and lay its little warm, pitching, kicking form in the cradle. They love and continue to love it. They love it because it is alive.

There never was a doll made anywhere by the most skillful artist, even the most beautifully made and human-looking thing, that could bring out the shining-eyed wonder in a couple's faces that a newborn baby can bring out. It does not have to be pretty; it just has to be their baby, alive, warm and breathing. There is no difference between this mechanical 'nickel-in-the-slot' Christianity passing for Christianity now and that Christianity of our fathers, where men worshipped God in awful wonder and adoration.

Bishop James Usher would go down by the bank of the river on a Saturday and spend the afternoon on his knees in the presence of God in awesome worship. Jonathan Edwards' son-in-law, David Brainerd, would kneel in the snow and be so lost in worship, prayer and intercession that when he was through the snow would be melted around him in a wide circle. John Fletcher, the saint of Methodism, used to kneel in his little bare room on the floor. When he had lived out his life and gone to be with God, they found that he had made a concave place in the floor where his knees actually wore out the boards. The walls in his room were stained with his breath where he had waited on God and where he had worshiped his God in the beauty of holiness.

I am very careful when I use the word 'adore'. I refuse to say about any person, 'Oh, I adore him,' or 'I adore her.' I love babies, I love people, but I never adore them. Personally, I use the word adoration for the only one who deserves it. In no other presence and before no other being can I kneel in fear, wonder and yearning and

121

feel the sense of possessiveness that cries 'mine, mine'. There are those who are so theologically stilted that they feel it is not right to say 'mine'.

I have gone through hymnbooks and in some I have seen where the editors edited the hymns of Wesley and Watts. They replaced the 'I's and the 'me's and the 'mine's and they put 'ours'. 'I love thee, O God' is changed to 'We love thee, O God.'

Because they are so modest they cannot imagine saying 'I', but you will find in worship they cry out, 'O God thou art my God, early will I seek thee,' and so it becomes a love experience between God and me so that it's 'I' and not 'you'.

Paul was like that, and David and Isaiah and Moses and the rest. I desire to possess God; 'God is my God', 'the Lord is my shepherd, I shall not be in want. He makes me lie down in green pastures.'

Can you image what an editor would have done with that: 'the Lord is our shepherd, we shall not be in want. He makes us lie down in green pastures': that is togetherness, all right. Therefore, we will all lie down together, but nobody has anything that means 'I'. You can say 'God and I'; you cannot say 'us' and mean anything.

Until you have been able to meet God in loneliness of soul, you and God, as if there is nobody else in the world, you will never know what it is to love other people in the world.

This adoration is the desire to be poured out at God's feet; we desire it, we want to be poured out at God's feet. When trying to elude King Saul, David got a touch of homesickness and said, 'Oh that I might have a drink out of the good old well of Bethlehem, as in my day of boyhood.' One of his men, looking for a promotion, started for the well (risking his life), got some water and brought it back to David. David picked up the cup and said, 'I can't drink this; this is blood. This cost you the rest of your life,' and he poured it out as a drink offering to God.

David knew God enough, had a boundless confidence in God's character, and came to admire him and love him for his excellence. Consecration is not hard for the person who has met God. This person insists on giving themselves entirely to God.

The list I have described has these factors in varying degrees of intensity, of course. They condition our thoughts, our words and our deeds. They hallow every place, time and set, and give back the glory that Christ had before the world. To the Christian, 'we in him and he in us and the glory he had, I have given unto them.'

I read of a creature God created who sealed up the sun, which was filled with wisdom and physical beauty, in Ezekiel 28:14–16.

The Old Testament tells that somewhere out there, beyond where the farthest rocket can go, God had a cherub created for that purpose. He was a creature created without embarrassment or fear, burning in the presence of God covering the stones of fire before the throne. He fell in love with his own beauty and God said, 'You are profane.' Most Bible teachers believe that is the devil.

The creature was created to worship; he turned his worship on himself and God cast him down.

My concern is that, unless we have a real spiritual awakening and Jesus tarries a while longer, we shall need missionaries from Africa or China to reintroduce North America to Christianity. God has no particular fondness for nations or buildings or denominations. He longs to be worshiped. When the church loses its love, it becomes sick.

We are born to worship and, if we are not worshiping God in the beauty of holiness, we have missed the reason for being born. Worship is a delightful, awesome, humbling, wonderful experience which we can have in varying degrees but have all those; you can live in the middle of it. You never need to leave church if you are worshipers. We can lock the building and be driven away from the place and leave it dark, but we have not left church at all. We carry our sanctuary with us; we never leave it.

If you know your heart is cold, it is not a hard heart yet; God has not rejected it. Therefore, if there is a yearning within, God put that yearning there. He did not put it there to mock you; he put it there that you might rise to it. God puts the bait of yearning in your heart. He does not turn his back on you; he puts it there because he is there, smiling, to meet you. Decide now that you are going to get ahead of this spiritually cold way of living.

A wonderful hymn, translated by Wesley, expresses this thought better than anything I can think of.

Jesus, Thy boundless love to me
No thought can reach, no tongue declare;
Unite my thankful heart with Thee
And reign without a rival there.
To Thee alone, dear Lord, I live;
Myself to Thee, dear Lord, I give.

Jesus, Thy boundless love to me
(Paul Gerhardt, 1607–1676,
translated by John Wesley)

Prayer:

Our Father, we praise you that your love is indeed boundless. Our wretchedness thankfully has great bounds established by your grace and is overcome by the boundlessness of your love. Grant to my heart a true sense of your presence, I pray, in Jesus' name. Amen.

CHAPTER 9

The Mystery of True Worship

In examining the subject of worship, I cannot emphasize enough that mystery surrounds this, and happy is the Christian who penetrates and breaks through this mystery. True Christian worship does not rise or fall according to human will, for there is only one object of worship worthy of humanity and that is God. I wish I could adequately describe the glory of the object we are to worship. If we could set forth the thousand attributes of a God who is dwelling in unapproachable light where no mortal can see him and live, fully eternal, omniscient, omnipotent and sovereign, we would be greatly humbled. God's people are not as humble as they ought to be and I believe this is why we do not truly see God in his sovereignty.

We are instructed to worship God, and I wonder how it could be that we Christians would fall on our knees before a man and say, 'Your throne, O God, is for ever and ever.' That man does not exist before whom I will kneel and say, 'God', with one lone supreme exception: the man Christ Jesus. He is the man whom the prophets saw in the vision and addressed by saying, 'Your throne, O God.'

All mystery has an ambience of confusion about it. How can we get out of this state of confusion if there is one God and no other? And how can we say Jesus Christ is a man yet we are taught never to worship man? How can we get down on our knees before him and worship? Here is the great mystery; I stand bareheaded before it, kneel, take my shoes off my feet before this burning bush and confess that I do not understand it. This mystery envelops my heart and I bow down in reverence and submission.

Simply put, the mystery is that God and man are united in one person, not two persons. All that is God and all that is man are fused eternally, inexplicitly and inseparably in the man Jesus Christ. When we kneel before the man Christ Jesus, we are in fact kneeling before God.

The Old Testament illustrates this with Moses before the burning bush. The fire burned in the bush, and the bush was not consumed. Moses instinctively knelt before the bush and worshiped God. Moses understood that God was in the bush. The bush was ordinary until God's presence permeated it and set it aflame. Moses could have been charged with idolatry by those who could not see the fire in the bush. They could not know the fire he was worshiping was none other than Jehovah.

Suppose there had been some Israelite who knew the teaching from Abraham that one God alone is to be worshiped. Suppose they had seen this man kneeling before a bush with his face in his hands, hiding his face, but they had not been able to see the fire. They would say, and rightly so, 'What do you mean by worshiping a bush? You are an idolater. Don't you know the Scripture?'

Of course, Moses would have known better. He knew the Scripture but he knew what the others did not know. He knew that the bush and the fire were united and infused there before him. They were essentially one. There was the nature of the bush and then there was the nature of Jehovah fused into one object. The bush was not consumed and Moses worshiped not the bush but the God who dwelt in the bush. Therefore, he knelt before that bush.

I admit that is an imperfect and inadequate illustration, for as soon as the fire departed from the bush it was just a bush again and no one could kneel and worship that bush ever again.

This was a picture of the coming of Christ. Christ Jesus was indeed God with all of the full implications of deity. Although Jesus was man in the perfect sense of the word, he was also God in the perfect sense of the word. Jesus Christ in the New Testament is the equivalent of the Old Testament burning bush. The striking difference is that the burning bush was a temporary experience, whereas Jesus Christ is both God and man for all eternity.

There was never any departure except for that awful moment on the cross when he said, 'My God, My God, why have you forsaken me?' He took all of the putrefying terrible mass of our sin on his holy self and died there. God turned his back on him but the deity and the humanity never parted and they remain today united in that one man. When we kneel before that man and say,

'My Lord and my God, your throne, O God, is for ever and ever,' we are talking to God for by the mystery of the hypostatic union man has become God and God has become man in the person of the Son, Jesus Christ.

We worship this person in mystery and wonder. We worship not man but God in the flesh.

If I did not believe the Bible for any other reason, I would believe it for the 45th Psalm and the 53rd chapter of Isaiah. I would see how the prophets foresaw down the centuries and proclaimed the great mystery of the one called Christ. These men of God describe him as radiantly beautiful and romantic and as a winsome deity. They said of him that he was fair, he was royal, he was gracious, he was majestic, he was true, and he was meek, righteous, loving, glad and fragrant. Human language was exhausted in trying to set forth the opulence of this one we call Christ, and after a while even the prophets gave up trying to describe him.

If I were searching the dictionary to find words to describe something or somebody I would be glad to kneel before this; here it is. He is fair and he is kingly, and yet he is gracious. Not a king who stands on his dignity and looks down his nose at the world, but a gracious king. His graciousness does not take away from his majesty; he is true and he is meek. Meekness and majesty. I would like to write a hymn or a book about it or maybe paint a picture or compose music about it, the meekness and majesty of Jesus. You do not find meekness and majesty united very much. The meekness was his humanity and the majesty was his deity. He was a human being like any other human being but he was God, and in his meekness he stood before Herod and before Pilate. And when he comes down from the sky it will be in his majesty, the majesty of God, and yet it will be the majesty of the man who is God.

Our Lord Jesus Christ is majestic and meek. Before his foes he stands in majesty, and before his friends he bows in meekness. You can experience whichever side you want. If you do not choose the meek side of Jesus, you will experience the majestic side of Jesus. The harlots came to him, and the babies, and the publicans, and the sick, and the bleeding woman, and the devil-possessed man. They came from everywhere, touched him and found him so meek that his power went out to them and healed them.

Fused in the person of Christ is all the beauty and wonderment of God, enabling us to worship God in the beauty of holiness. The tremendous aspect of this worship is that we can worship God wherever Jesus is. Wherever we find him is the perfect place to worship. I cannot explain this mystery; I only can revel in it and kneel before this eternal burning bush.

Why is it that when we think of worship we think of something we do when we go to church? God's poor stumbling, bumbling people, how confused we can get – and stay confused for a lifetime and die confused. Books are written that confuse us further and we write songs to confirm the books and confuse ourselves further still and we do it all as if the only place we can worship God is in a church building that we call the house of God. We enter the house dedicated to God, made out of bricks, linoleum and other stuff, and we say, 'The Lord is in his holy temple; let all kneel before him.'

I personally enjoy starting a service that way occasionally. But it does not stop here. Come 9.00 Monday morning, if you do not walk into your office and say, 'the Lord is in my office and the entire world is silent before him,' then you were not worshiping the Lord on Sunday. If you cannot worship him on Monday, you did not worship him on Sunday. If you do not worship him on Saturday, your worship on Sunday was not authentic. Some people put God in a box they call the church building. God is not present in church any more than he is present in your home. God is not here any more than he is in your factory or office.

As a young Christian, I worked for the B.F. Goodrich Company in Akron, Ohio, helping to make rubber tires. I worshiped God at my assembly-line station until I had tears in my eyes. Nobody ever saw the tears or asked me about them but I would not have hesitated to tell them why. As I went along and worked a while at something it became automatic – soon you can do it and think about something else. Some daydream; I worshiped. I got to the point where I could do my work with passing skill and then I could worship God at the same time. God was at my work just as much as he was at my church. As far as I was concerned there was no difference. If God is not in your factory, if God is not in your store, if God is not in your office, then God is not in your church when you go there. When we worship our God, the breath of songs on earth starts the organs playing in heaven above.

The total life, the whole man and the whole woman, must worship God. Faith, love, obedience, loyalty, conduct and life, all of these are to worship God. If there is anything in you that does not worship God, then there is nothing in you that worships God very well. If you compartmentalize your life and let certain parts worship God but other parts not worship God, then you are not worshiping God as you should. It is a great delusion we fall into, the idea that in church or in the presence of death or in the midst of sublimity is the only setting for worship.

You carry worship inside your heart. You can have your worship with you. I have been with people who became very spiritual when standing on a mountain and looking down. I remember being caught in a storm one time in the mountains in Pennsylvania and looking out from there. I don't remember how many miles they told us it was, I think it was fifty from where we were, but you could see out of it. We huddled up against a rock while the storm and the hailstones hit us. They came rattling and roaring down on us and we huddled next to the car against the rock as that great storm writhed in its white fury over the mountain.

I do not have to see a storm on a mountain to make me know how jealous God is. The stars in their courses tell about it and the baby that cries tells about it, the flower that blooms by the wayside tells about it, and the fine snow that drifted down tells about it. We do not have to have it dramatically brought home to us for it to be true.

It is a great delusion to think that because we feel a sense of the poetic in the presence of storm or stars or mountains that we are spiritual. That is not necessarily true at all, because murderers, tyrants and drunkards also can feel like that.

There never was a drunkard who did not have such feelings when he came to himself, and there never was a tyrant who, after giving the command to slay a dozen men, on his way home might see something that would draw poetic worship from him. That is not imagined; that is worship.

Worship pleasing to God saturates our whole being. There is no worship pleasing to God until there is nothing in me that is displeasing to God. I cannot compartmentalize my life, worship God on Sunday and not worship him on Monday; worship him in my songs and displease him in my business engagements. I cannot worship God in silence in the church on Sunday to the sound of hymns, then go out on the next day and be displeasing to him in my activities. No worship is wholly pleasing to God until there is nothing in us that is displeasing to God.

Without Jesus Christ there is no goodness, and so I do not apologize at all when I say that your worship has to be all-inclusive and take in all of you. If you are not worshiping God in all of your life, you are not worshiping him acceptably in any area of your life.

Although worship is a natural desire of Christians, there are disciplines we must employ. I believe personal preparation is essential in our worship of God. That preparation is not always a pleasant thing and must include some revolutionary changes in our life. Some things must be destroyed in our life. The gospel of Jesus Christ is not only constructive but also destructive, destroying certain elements in us that should not be there, things that impede worship. The fire in the burning bush consumed only those elements that should not have been there. And so, as we yield ourselves to the operations of the Holy Spirit, he will begin rooting out those elements in our life that impede worship that is both satisfying to us and acceptable to God.

For example, many are hampered in their worship by the inclusion of magic. Certain words and phrases carry some magical essence for some people. There is no magic in faith and no magic in the name of Jesus. Reciting certain phrases or even certain special verses of Scripture has no miraculous effect in our life. This is what the Bible refers to as 'vain repetition'.

Some may think they are worshiping in the name of Jesus but they are not necessarily worshiping in the nature of Jesus. Name and nature are one in the Bible. It is impossible to divide Jesus between name and nature. When we ask anything in the name of Jesus, it does not mean pronouncing the name, J E S U S. It means we are in conformity to his nature. To chant the name 'Jesus' has no power in it. Whoever asks after his nature and asks in accordance to his word, that person can get what they want.

I cannot live contrary to the nature of Jesus on Monday and then on Monday night when I face a crisis get on my knees and call on the name of Jesus and think that there is some magic in that name. I would be disappointed and disillusioned, for if I am not living in that name I cannot pray properly in that name. If I am not living in that nature, I cannot pray rightfully in that nature. We cannot live according to our nature and worship according to his. When his nature and ours begin to harmonize under the influence of the Holy Spirit, the power of his name begins to be felt. The same mystery that united Jesus with God also unites us with Jesus.

The Bible clearly teaches, 'But we have the mind of Christ' (1 Corinthians 2:16).

Then Paul says, 'To them God has chosen to make known among the Gentiles the glorious riches of this mystery, which is Christ in you, the hope of glory' (Colossians 1:27).

I know the name of Jesus is far above all the names of all kings and queens and archangels and presidents and prime ministers. Above Moses, Aaron, and all who have ever had honor in the entire world. I know that at the 'name of Jesus, every knee shall bow and every tongue confess that he is Lord, to the glory of God the Father'. And, 'he will ride down the sky and he will call to the nations of the earth, and they will come before him and he will be their judge supreme'. I also know that we cannot take advantage of that name by any twisted religious magic. We have to live in that name and you cannot rest until every area in your total life rests in God, and everything honors God.

Does your business honor God? Are you living it yourself? If it does not honor God then I cannot see you living for God and honoring him. If your business does not honor God, you cannot honor God. You are buying and selling. You cut corners, you push and scream and you cannot possibly please God.

What about your relations with the opposite sex? How can we worship God if our relations with the opposite sex are such that God is displeased? I am not a prude, but I believe our relationships with one another ought to be right and pure in every way.

I wonder about the relationships in your home life and your school life and your use of money and time. Is all this pleasing to God? Some imagine their time is their own and they can do with it as they please. Your time is not your own; it belongs to the God who created time.

If God gives you a few more years, remember they are not yours. Your time must honor God, your home must honor God, your activity must honor God and everything about you must honor God.

If you want to die right then you have to live right, and if you want to be right when you are old then you have to be right when you are young.

You are not worshiping right in any place until you are worshiping God right in every place. If you cannot worship him in the kitchen, you cannot worship him audibly in the church.

There is a current idea that Christians can serve God at their own convenience: how utterly terrible, how awful. Do we seem to be the followers of the one who had nowhere to lay his head until he laid it back against the cross and died? So we need that time for preparation, testing and choosing. Thank God, there is time; I do not know when time will be called on us, but there is still time now.

Worship is not a spotlight focusing on one area of our life. True worship, worship pleasing to God, radiates throughout a person's entire life.

Prayer:

O God, we humble ourselves before that mystery uniting us with you. We worship you not according to our understanding, which is inadequate, but we worship you in spirit and truth. We honor you in our hearts, bow before that sacred burning bush and hide our faces in reverential fear. In Jesus' name. Amen.

CHAPTER 10

The Natural Dwelling Place of God

John 4:23

True worship accords with the nature of God. By that, I mean we worship God according to what God is and not according to what he is not. The frightful error of idolatry and the reason God hates it so is that it is worship according to what God is not. He said about the Samaritans, 'You do not know what you worship; you worship according to what God is not. We Jews know what we worship.' Salvation was of the Jews not because they were better than other people, because they were not. Their prophets said distinctly that they were worse than some people were, but God chose to reveal the truth to them and gave them the oracles. By such revelation, God made it possible for Israel to worship according to the nature of God. And Jesus Christ our Lord says that God is spirit and we worship according to that nature of God.

In light of this, we must keep in mind that God is not affected by the attributes of matter. He is not affected by weight, size or space. A well-taught Christian knows that the great God is not affected by space, as he contains space in his bosom. The well-instructed Christian knows God is not affected by speed. God gets around all points and so we worship God. God is spirit, God is not affected by location, God is not some place to which you come and recede but God is all about us and contains space and so he is as near to one place as he is to another. It is a great comfort to know that God is as near to one place as he is to another place.

Because God made us in his image, there is a part of us that is like God. The human soul is the most like God of anything that has ever been created, and uniquely corresponds to God.

How can this be? There is so much sin in the world and so much that seems so ungodly. The simple answer is sin. Because humankind has fallen does not mean that what is fallen does not have about it yet the luminance of the likeness of God. It is easy for God to restore us and redeem us, because God has material to work with that was once made in his image.

Let us bring in an Old Testament illustration. Suppose a potter is making a beautiful clay pot. While spinning on the wheel, it runs into some sand or grit and falls apart. There it is now, broken and no longer useful. But the material out of which it is made, although it doesn't look like a teapot anymore, and there is no artistry there and the soul of the artist is not in it and cannot be in it because it has been broken on the wheel, can still fairly easily be taken up by the potter again. He can take out the offending parts and make it into another vessel. He could not do that if he had iron, he could not do it if he had rock, but he can do it with clay because clay is the material with which he works. It was broken the first time, but he can restore it using the same material.

God made us in his image and while we are not altogether clear about what that image of God is, we do know that the human soul relates to and responds to God. In the temptation in the garden, human beings fell apart and lost the artistry, the beauty, and the holiness of God. But they did not lose the potential to become godlike again if they got into the hands of the divine artist.

This is the purpose in redemption. Taking on the material of fallen humanity and, by the mystery of regeneration and sanctification, restoring it again so that people are like God and like Christ. This is why we preach redemption. That is what redemption is: it is not saving us from hell although it does save us from hell, but, more importantly, it is making it so that we can be like God again.

How does this take place?

First, nobody can worship without the Holy Spirit. God is spirit, the Holy Spirit is the Spirit of God, and therefore the Holy Spirit is the only one who can properly lead the heart to worship God acceptably. The fallen human mind does not know how to worship God acceptably so the Holy Spirit takes the fallen human mind, points it up, corrects it, purges it, aims it and directs it so that it is worshiping God. That is why it is so vastly and vitally important that we should know the Holy Spirit.

I have often felt like getting on my knees and apologizing to the Holy Spirit for the way the church has treated him. We have treated him shoddily and in a poor way. We have treated him in such a manner that, if you were to treat a guest that way, the guest would slip away grief-stricken and never return. We have treated the Holy Spirit wretchedly. He is God himself, the link binding the Father and the Son, and is the substance uncreated, which is deity. Yet the Holy Spirit is typically ignored in the average church, even in the average gospel church.

How many go to church on a Sunday counting on the Holy Spirit being present? How many really count on the Holy Spirit speaking to them? How many trust the Holy Spirit to take on a human voice and speak through it? That he is going to take a human ear and listen through it?

This idea that anybody can offer worship is all wrong. The view that we can worship while ignoring the Spirit is all wrong. To crowd the Spirit into a corner and ignore him, quench him, resist him and yet worship God acceptably is a great heresy, which needs correcting. Only the Holy Spirit knows how to worship God acceptably.

In the book of Romans (8:26), you will find that only the Holy Spirit knows how to pray. It says in verse 26, 'In the same way, the Spirit helps us in our weakness. We do not know what we ought to pray for, but the Spirit himself intercedes for us with groans that words cannot express. And he who searches our hearts knows the mind of the Spirit, because the Spirit intercedes for the saints in accordance with God's will.' In our prayers, there will be mutterings and repetition until the Holy Spirit takes them, purges them, cleanses them and makes them acceptable to God through Jesus Christ our mediator.

Therefore, it is impossible to pray without the Spirit. The most powerful prayers are prayed in the Spirit and we cannot worship without the Holy Spirit. Either we ignore him or we exploit him for our personal pleasure and entertainment. I think it is time the church rethought this whole matter of the place of the Holy Spirit in the church of our Lord Jesus Christ. We should rethink it in the light of the Scriptures because, without the Holy Spirit, we are like Israel when she continued worshiping God after the fire left the holy place and there was no Shekinah, no glory, no fire, no light and no presence there. Yet Israel continued to worship, vainly and futilely. Pitifully they continued to worship, forgetting that the Spirit of worship had left them long ago.

Spirituality is one of the ingredients of worship and, without spirituality, I cannot worship God in a manner acceptable to him, no matter how much I worship. If it is not acceptable worship then it is vain worship and better not attempted.

The second ingredient in worship is sincerity, as distinct from formality or duplicity. We have extreme and heinous examples of this, taught by our missionaries. The missionaries tell us about the heathen who worshiped their god and they liked to cheat him.

You do not have to go to some pagan society to see this. Some have become quite brazen in this. We make promises to God that we do not intend to keep, thinking we can get from God what we want. We think we can cheat the Lord by crossing our fingers and meaning something else and the Lord will not hear, will not notice us. We have to be absolutely sincere if we are going to worship God, which is distinct from formality. I do not know whether anything done merely formally has any meaning at all. It is possible to take part in religious ritual and not even know what we are doing or why we are doing it; we are just going through meaningless motions and repeating empty words and phrases.

The Lord pointed to a little child and said that the little child was an example. I believe that one thing about a little child is complete sincerity. No matter how embarrassingly he or she may be talking, how many embarrassing things he or she may be saying, a child is nevertheless absolutely sincere. And it is this sincerity that we must cultivate prayerfully if our worship is to be accepted by Almighty God.

What a terrible thing it is to spend a lifetime making offerings to the Almighty, all of which are rejected. Cain made his offering to the Almighty, God did not answer and would not accept it, and Cain's countenance fell.

Honesty is the third ingredient. It must be in all our prayers, as distinct from mere propriety. I suppose honesty and sincerity are twin brothers and cannot be separated, although they are separate and not identical. But there must be complete honesty before God. If I get on my knees and pray, 'Lord, meet our missionary budget,' and the Lord knows I am not going to give anything toward it, he knows I am praying dishonestly.

If I pray, 'Lord, save this man,' but I have never done anything about sharing my faith with him, I'm dishonest. If I ask God to do things that I could do for myself, I am dishonest in my praying. But we have glossed over it until it sounds shocking to hear it said. It is true nevertheless.

Fourthly, we must have simplicity in worship as distinct from sophistry and sophistication.

I have heard a few people pray in my time who were utterly simple, almost embarrassingly simple. They were so simple-hearted that one tended to feel perhaps they were not intellectually strong. But there is no incompatibility between intellectual power and simplicity of heart. Jesus Christ our Lord was simple, to the point of being direct in his relationships. To our old Quaker friends who lived generations ago, simplicity was everything.

When the old English Quakers went before the king they would not take off their broad-brimmed hats because they thought that was giving too much honor to a man. They would do anything before God but insisted on wearing those hats, and looked out of many a set of bars in many a prison just for that reason. Personally, I do not think there would be any harm in it; I would take my hat off. There is nothing wrong with uncovering your head. You are certainly not worshiping anybody, but the point is that they believed and acted according to what they believed, and God honored them for living by their faith. Simplicity; utter simplicity. They said 'thee' and 'thou' and they called each other Mary and John, or whatever the name was, and they taught the church of Christ to be simple.

If we were ever to break ourselves down and suddenly be faced with death or some other tragedy or terror, we would be forced to see how unnatural we are and how unlike ourselves. We have lived like zoo lions, utterly unlike the lions that roam the wilds of Africa, and so we are in this civilization of ours, pressed on every side.

There must be simplicity before going to pray or worship God. You must worship God simply and I do not care who you are or what you are; it must be simple.

It takes simplicity and humility to worship God acceptably. Most of us are half a dozen people. I have four or five reputations. To some people I am this, to some people I am that, and I suppose everybody is the same. When we try to live up to our reputations, it is always difficult and we always get into trouble.

Then, fifthly, true worship must be internal: internality as distinct from externalism. We ought to thank God from the depths of our hearts that we do not need any machinery to worship him. We can worship God in spirit and in truth through the depths of our own heart just as well as the angels in glory can worship God. We do not have to have anything; we do not have to die with a crucifix in our hand, or any other religious artifact.

Anything may mean something to a worshiping heart and it can mean nothing if the heart is not worshiping. A wedding ring may mean a great deal to a woman but only because she believes it tells her something about a man, not because it has any intrinsic value. If she loses it down the sink she will be a little sad, but she will not lose her husband. She will not lose that for which the ring stood – his love; she can get another ring. Therefore, worship is an internal thing.

My personal worship tells something about God

and me. I can worship truly, because something is true between God and me. If, after years of going to the same church, I come to associate that church with worshiping God, that is natural, that is psychological, that is a conditioned reflex; I think they call it that in psychology. But it does not mean that if I do not go to that church again or the church burns down, then I cannot worship God.

I believe it is time that illuminating persons begin the arduous task of reforming Christian worship. And as we begin to understand it again in the church of Christ, I believe it will bring revival to us.

Back to our basic text: 'The king is enthralled by your beauty; honor him, for he is your Lord.'

The soul is a God-shaped void. If I were to carry it further, I would say our soul is a God-shaped garment, like a glove shaped to fit our hand. God cannot enter because it is full of rubbish. Try putting a lot of junk in the glove sometime and then try placing your hand into it; you cannot do it. That glove must be empty before a hand can go into it.

The heart must be empty before God can enter. That is why at the altars in times of evangelism and prayer and under pressure to get people right with God we insist on an emptying-out of ourselves. Your soul is a God-shaped garment and God wants to clothe himself with it. But he cannot enter because there is rubbish in it. Search your heart and find out how much rubbish you have collected over the past years. How much moral rubbish, how much intellectual rubbish, how much rubbish of habit, of custom, of things you do and do not do, think and do not think. You must empty it all out.

I would like to say I have found some new way, but there is no new way. Empty the rubbish out of your soul, turn yourself to God in the name of the Lord Jesus Christ and he will fill you, and come in and clothe himself with you. Only the garment is unclean and God will not wear an unclean garment. God wants to wear a pure garment.

Once we have emptied ourselves of everything, we must be cleansed. Only through the blood of the Lamb can that emptied soul be cleansed so God can enter. An emptied and cleansed soul is the natural dwelling place of God. So let us ask God to cleanse us. We can empty ourselves but we can never cleanse ourselves.

If you have something in you preventing God from entering, you can empty that out. But if after you are empty you are still unclean, you can never cleanse yourself. Only God can do that by the blood of the everlasting covenant, by the fire of the Holy Spirit and by the discipline of obedience. God cleanses his people and makes them white and pure in the blood of the Lamb.

Everybody who knows about birds knows they have what are called natural habitats. You do not go to a swamp to find a wood thrush. If you want to hear a wood thrush, you go to the cool woods when the shadows fall. Go there and wait for the evening to come and then the wood thrush will come. Quiet at first and then louder and bolder, and as the shadows grow deeper she will play her lovely flute in the darkness. She will never go to the swamp.

If you want to hear a red-winged blackbird make its 'clump, clumping' sound, you do not go to the cool woods in the evening; you go to the swampy land where the cattails slip their brown flowers up. There you will find the red-winged blackbird.

If you want to hear a wren sing you do not go to the woods and you do not go to the swamp; go to your own backyard and there she will be, singing with delight. It is what they call the natural habitat.

I believe that the Holy Spirit has a natural habitat. By habitat, I mean he makes himself at home, heard, or felt where he can speak and where he can live. That natural habitat is nothing else but the soul of a person.

You ask how such a thing can be. Because God made that soul in the image of God and God can dwell in his own image without embarrassment. And just as the blackbird can sing among the cattails and just as the rabbit can hop among the briars and just as the wood thrush can sing unseen at the edge of the woods at night, so the Holy Spirit wants to come into your soul and live in it. Not weekending there, not a houseguest for a while, but making your soul a permanent habitation.

Only sin can prevent that, which is why worship and sin are incompatible. That is why you cannot deal with the matter of true worship and omit the question of sin. Sin can prevent worship. You cannot worship God with unconfessed sin reigning in your heart. 'Here I am! I stand at the door and knock. If anyone hears my voice and opens the door, I will come in and eat with him, and he with me' (Revelation 3:20). Here is the picture of Jesus in your house, dwelling with you. 'I will come in, unto you. I will take you unto me but I will come in unto you.' Jesus desires to be in the house of his friend – your house.

Your soul is a God-shaped glove. God wants to enter into it but it is full of rubbish. Get rid of the rubbish and you will not have to beg God to come in.

The old-fashioned light bulb was made in such a way that at the end was a little projection. When pumped empty it became a vacuum. As a kid, I used to take a pair of pliers and break that little projection off and there was a popping sound as 14 lb per square inch of atmospheric pressure rushed into that bulb. You did not have to get in the bulb and get on your knees, beg and say, 'Please come, atmosphere, please come in.' All you had to do was take away the obstruction and the atmosphere rushed in. Nature abhors a vacuum.

The human soul is a vacuum and we have filled it with trash. As far as God is concerned, we have only to empty it and God rushes in, cleanses it and fills it. Not for us but for himself, and he does not have to be begged. The most natural thing in the universe is for the Creator to indwell the human soul.

> *Thou who givest of Thy gladness*
> *Till the cup runs o'er –*
> *Cup whereof the pilgrim weary*
> *Drinks to thirst no more –*
> *Not a-nigh me, but within me*
> *Is Thy joy divine;*

Thou, O Lord, hast made Thy dwelling
In this heart of mine.

The Indwelling Christ
Gerhard Tersteegen (1697–1769)

Prayer:
Eternal God, who dwells in the heavens above us, we humbly bow before you with anxious thoughts of fellowship with you. We thank you that you have been enough for us. Our thirsty hearts have been satiated in you. Amen.

CHAPTER 11

The Worthy Object
of Worship

Song of Songs 5:8–16

This passage in the Song of Songs is a parable of our relationship with this one called the shepherd. It details the
marvelous details of that relationship. Our Lord is the
shepherd, the redeemed church is the fair bride and, in
an hour of distress, she tells the daughters of Jerusalem
among whom she lives, 'If you find my lover, tell him I
am faint with love.' Naturally they inquire, 'How is your
beloved better than others, that you charge us so?'

The world has a perfect right to ask that question of
the church. If the church is going to say that the Lord is
worthy and a worthy lover then the world has a right to
ask what kind of lover he is. Why should you be promot-
ing him; 'How is your beloved better than others?'

Others are offered up for the world's admiration and
worship, so why this one? What qualities recommend
him to them?

In the book of Psalms, David also talks about this.
'My heart is stirred by a noble theme as I recite my verses
for the king; my tongue is the pen of a skillful writer.
You are the most excellent of men and your lips have

been anointed with grace, since God has blessed you for ever… All your robes are fragrant with myrrh and aloes and cassia; from palaces adorned with ivory the music of the strings makes you glad.' This 45th psalm is a rapt description of this shepherd king wooing the young bride to himself. Ask Peter that question and he will say, 'He is Lord of all.'

It is important to consider the object of our worship, which is none other than the Lord himself, the Lord, our righteousness, the Lord Jesus Christ. He is the Lord of all, and in order that we might get it straight in our minds we need to know what he is Lord of and why we should love him. This is a fair consideration.

Why is he more than any other man and, furthermore, why should we worship him?

We can worship Jesus Christ the man without idolatry because he is also God. By the mystery of the theanthropic union, he has united humanity with deity. Jesus Christ is both divine and human in nature and has taken humanity up into God so that he himself is God. He has joined in the beauty and wonder of the theanthropic union of God and man in one so that whatever God is, Christ is. Therefore, Jesus could truthfully say, 'Anyone who has seen me has seen the Father' (John 14:9).

Our confidence is that, when we worship the Lord Jesus, we are not displeasing the Father for we are worshiping the Father in him. This is the mystery of the theanthropic union, joining us forever to God through the Lord Jesus Christ.

I will divide it a little bit so that we can understand

it better. Let me begin with a marvelous hymn by Oliver Wendell Holmes (1809–1894).

LORD of all being, throned afar,
Thy glory flames from sun and star;
Center and soul of every sphere,
Yet to each seeking heart how near!

The hymn-writer did not say, 'He is the Lord of all beings', but he is the 'Lord of all being', which is something else, and something more. He is the Lord of all actual existence. He is the Lord of all kinds of beings, the Lord of all spiritual being and all natural being and all physical being. He is the Lord of all being and when we worship him, we encompass all being.

Some give themselves up to the disciplines of science, technology, philosophy, art and music. When we worship the Lord Jesus Christ, we embrace and encompass all disciplines because he is the Lord of them all. Therefore, he is the Lord of all being and the enemy of all not being, and he is the Lord of all life.

These statements are fundamental to any correct understanding that he is the Lord of all life. It is written in 1 John, that word of life, which was with the Father and dwells among us. ('The life appeared; we have seen it and testify to it, and we proclaim to you the eternal life, which was with the Father and has appeared to us,' 1 John 1:2.)

Charles Wesley understood this and put it in his immortal hymn, 'Jesus, lover of my soul'.

155

Plenteous grace with Thee is found,
Grace to cover all my sin;
Let the healing streams abound;
Make and keep me pure within.
Thou of life the fountain art,
Freely let me take of Thee;
Spring Thou up within my heart;
Rise to all eternity.

He is the Lord of all life and thus also the Lord of all the essential possibilities of life. He is the Lord of all kinds of life.

All of creation is populated with many kinds of life. In the spring, the buds will come out, promising floral life all over; he is the Lord of that kind of life. Spring will bring back the birds; the rabbits will be out and you will see the animals. That is another kind of life and he is the Lord of that kind of life.

Then we have intellectual life: the life of imagination and reason, and he is the Lord of that kind of life.

And we have the spiritual life, and he is the Lord of that kind of life. He is the Lord of angels; he is the Lord of the cherubim and seraphim, so he is the Lord of all life and he is the Lord of all sorts of life.

So, in response to the inquiry, 'How is your beloved better than others?', we can say: 'He is Lord of all.'

Further, the Holy Spirit says, 'He is the Lord of all wisdom.' All deep eternal wisdom lies in Jesus Christ as a treasure hidden away, and no wisdom exists outside of him. All the deep eternal purposes of God are in him because his perfect wisdom enables him to plan ahead. All history is the slow development of his purposes.

This is difficult to justify in light of the world around us. Today, all we see are the laborers in creation at work. We see the laborers working on the external scaffolding and things do not look very beautiful now. Any building in the process of construction will not possess the beauty of its finished state.

Whether they know it or not, these laborers are doing the will of God and are bringing things about. The individual workers may not have the finished picture in mind, only the small area they are working on at the time; however, they are moving the project to its final state of completion, fulfilling the will of the general contractor. Even the devil, unwittingly, fulfills God's will. God is making all evil men as well as all good men and all adverse things as well as all favorable things work for a bringing forth of his glory on the day when all shall be fulfilled in him (Romans 8:28).

Then, he is the Lord of all righteousness and all concepts of righteousness and all possibilities of righteousness. He is wisdom and righteousness and there is no getting around him. There is no book available on Christian ethics (or any other kind of ethics) that can tell you anything he does not already know and of which he is not already Lord. It is written in Hebrews 1:8, 'But about the Son he says, "Your throne, O God, will last for ever and ever, and righteousness will be the scepter of your kingdom. You have loved righteousness and hated wickedness; therefore God, your God, has set you above your companions by anointing you with the oil of joy."'

When the Old Testament high priest went into the holy of holies to offer sacrifices once a year, he wore a miter on his forehead. On that miter was engraved in Hebrew the words, 'Holiness unto the Lord.' This Jesus Christ, our Lord and high priest, is righteous and he is the Lord of righteousness.

He is also the Lord of all mercy, for he establishes his kingdom upon rebels.

First, he has to redeem them, win them and renew a right spirit within them, and all this he does. He is the Lord of all mercy, he is the Lord of all power and he transforms these rebels according to his righteousness.

God put something in the human heart making it capable of understanding and appreciating beauty. He put in us the love of harmonious forms, the love and appreciation of color and beautiful sounds. It is in everybody. He put in us also the love of moral forms of line and color. All things that are beautiful to the eye and the ear are only the external counterparts of that internal beauty which is moral beauty. There *is* such a thing as moral beauty.

It was foretold of Jesus Christ our Lord that he would have no beauty or majesty to attract us to him (Isaiah 53:2). Artists have painted Jesus with a tender feminine face and clear beautiful eyes and an open delightful countenance, with curly hair streaming down his shoulders. They have completely forgotten that the Bible declares that there was no beauty in him that we should desire him. They have forgotten that, when the high priests wanted to crucify him, they had to have an arrangement made to identify him. Judas Iscariot did not say, 'When we get there, pick out that beautiful one with a feminine face, curls down his back and the light on his face; pick him out, he is the one.' They were standing there with their typical Jewish haircuts and Hebrew garments, all looking alike, so Judas had to give them a signal: 'The one I kiss, that will be the one.' They did not recognize Jesus. When Jesus came, Judas passed by Peter, John, Philip and the rich man, kissed Jesus, and said, 'That's the man there.' If he had looked as beautiful physically as they paint him, why was it necessary for him to be betrayed with a kiss? He simply did not look like that; 'there was nothing in his appearance that we should desire him'.

The beauty of Jesus that has charmed the centuries is this moral beauty, which even his enemies acknowledge. Friedrich Nietzsche, the great German philosopher, perhaps the greatest nihilist and one of the greatest antichrists that ever lived in the world, died beating his forehead on the floor of his cell. He once said, 'That man Jesus I love, but I don't like Paul.' He did not like theology and he did not like to hear how we have to be saved and about the necessity of the new birth. In particular, he objected to justification by faith. However, there was something attractive about Jesus that he could not help but love.

So there is moral beauty in the Lord Jesus Christ and he is the Lord of all beauty of moral form and moral texture. He is the Lord of it all.

Sin has scarred the world and made it inharmonious

and unsymmetrical, and has filled hell with ugliness. If you love beautiful things, you had better stay out of hell, for hell will be the quintessence of all that is morally ugly. The spirit of things determines the external manifestation of that spirit and I believe hell will be the ugliest place in all God's creation. When rough men say something is as ugly as hell they are using a proper and valid comparison. Heaven is the place of harmonious numbers. Heaven is the place of loveliness, the place of beauty, because the one who is all beautiful is there. He is the Lord of all beauty and earth lies between all that is ugly in hell and all that is beautiful in heaven. Earth lies between it and you see the ugliness set over against the beauty.

Why is it like that? Why is there light and shadows? Why is there ugliness and beauty? Why is there so much good and so much bad? Why are there pleasant things and things that are tragic and hard to live with? It is because the earth lies halfway between heaven's beauty and hell's ugliness.

You say, 'Why are people capable of doing what they do?' The answer is because they lie halfway between heaven and hell.

Is there any Christian who has not been hurt by some other Christian, and maybe a real Christian too? Why is it that a person will be on their knees praying earnestly one day and another day will hurt another Christian? Because we stand halfway between heaven and hell. You and I must be pulled out of all this, and the Lord of beauty is saving his people from the ugliness of sin.

Our Lord Jesus Christ came into the world that he might save us from the ugliness of sin to a beautiful heaven.

The Old Testament gives us the story of a man named Isaac. His father, Abraham, called for his servant to go and find an acceptable bride for his son. With the help of the Holy Spirit, that old servant went down into the town Abraham indicated and found a young woman there. The Bible pictures her as very beautiful. Her name was Rebekah and she must have been beautiful, as the servant was instructed to find a bride that was beautiful to look at.

Isaac is a type of our Lord Jesus Christ. God the Father sent the Holy Spirit out among the people of the world to win a bride for Christ, one that was worthy of him. The bride's significance was to rest in the groom. She has no worth of her own but her worth lies in her relationship with the groom. Jesus Christ is the groom and is worthy of our love, adoration and joyful worship.

Rebekah was merely the daughter of her father. But when she was taken to Isaac she took on a new identity, the identity of her groom. Our identity is now in our groom. The past identity is forgotten, with all its obligations. Our groom is now our identity and nothing in our past matters any more. The bride takes on not only the identity of the groom but his name as well. She is now forever known by that name.

This groom shepherd is worthy of our affection and deserving of our leaving everything behind and embracing him as our own.

Prayer:

O God, in great humility we bow before you and take upon ourselves your name and your nature. Everything in our past is lost in glorious oblivion and all our future is wrapped up in you. We accept you as our groom shepherd and are eternally grateful that the gracious Spirit of God sought us out and brought us to you. We long for nothing else but you. Amen.

CHAPTER 12

The Authenticity of Ownership

During the first few years of my ministry, if I could not have prayed and asked God for things, I would have starved to death, dragging my wife and family down with me. So I believe in praying for things. I believe we can claim the promises of God to supply our daily needs. That is not all there is to Christianity, and it certainly represents the lowest section of it. Too many people are possessed by the idea of getting things from God to the extent of obscuring everything else.

There is so much more in the Christian life than getting things from God. Our personal relationship with Jesus Christ is the most important thing about us, and it is defined for us in the worship we offer to God. The important thing is the object of our worship and for the Christian that is none other than God, the Father of our Lord Jesus Christ. Because of the crucial nature of this, we must know who this one is that we are to worship.

The scripture says, 'He is the Lord of all wisdom and he is the Father of the everlasting ages.' Not the 'everlasting Father', as it says in the King James Version, but the 'Father of the everlasting ages'.

This Father lays out the ages as an architect would

lay out his blueprint or as a real-estate developer lays out a small town and then builds hundreds of houses in it. But God is not dealing with buildings and local developments. He is dealing with the ages and is the Lord of all wisdom. Because he is perfect in wisdom, he is able to do this and history is but the slow development of his purposes.

Take a house that is being built; the architect has drawn it down to the last tiny dot and X. He knows everything about it, has studied it thoroughly and writes his name at the bottom. The plans are now complete and he hands them over to the contractor, who farms the work out to the electrician and plumber and all the rest. The building process begins. In the beginning, it does not look too encouraging. Visit the site and you will wonder what it is going to be. It does not look like anything at the moment. It is a mess now, with a steam shovel in there with its great ugly nose digging out a hole and throwing earth up onto the bank or into trucks to haul away. They are unloading bricks over there and everything seems a confused conglomeration of this and that.

Come back six, eight, or ten months later, and you will see a charming house there with no signs of the confusion of construction. The landscapers have been in; the trees and the evergreens are standing there with their little green spikes by the windows and it is a beautiful thing.

We are now to believe that the Father of the everlasting ages, the Lord of all wisdom, has laid out his plan and is working toward a predetermined goal. But all we see is a church all mixed up and sorely distressed by schisms and rent asunder by heresies. We see it back-slidden in one part of the world, in confusion in another part, and we shrug our shoulders and wonder what is all this, who is behind all this? The answer is that he is the Lord of the ages, he is laying it all out, and what you are seeing now is only the steam shovel working, the truck backed up with bricks; that is all. We can see only workers in overalls going about killing time. You are just seeing people and people make you sick because of the way they do things. To the uninitiated, everything looks like confusion and turmoil, as though no one is in charge.

We backslide and tumble around and get mixed up and run after the Will o' the Wisp and think it is the Shekinah glory. We hear an owl hoot and think it is the silver trumpet and take off in the wrong direction and spend a century catching up on ourselves. Return in another millennium or so and see what the Lord of all wisdom has done with it. No matter how much of a mess it appears, God has a way of working everything out for his glory. He is the Lord of all wisdom and history is but the slow development of his purposes.

I am glad I am attached to something good. That there is something good somewhere in the universe. Despite appearances, behind all the mess of our world is the Lord of all wisdom sorting it out in his way and in his time.

I could not possibly be a Pollyanna-style optimist. I was born wrong. I would have to have had a different father and mother and a different ancestral line back at least ten generations for me to be a Pollyanna, a plum-pudding philosopher believing that everything is good. I cannot believe that. I do not think it is true. There is so much that is not right everywhere. We might as well admit it. Wickedness prevails on so many fronts that it would be impossible to ignore it.

Some religious people try to blank out all the negatives and concentrate on the positives. If you want to get ahead in life, they advise, ignore the negatives in your life and focus on the positive and in the end the positive will override all negatives.

But, if you take the Bible as your guide, righteousness is not found among us. If you think it is, then get on a bus somewhere when there's a crowd and you'll find that, no matter how old and feeble you are, you will get the rib or two, or at least get badly jolted by the elbow of some housewife on her way home. It is hard to concentrate on the positive with a sharp elbow in your side. And people are just not good. Among the first things we learn to do are something bad and something mean. The first word a baby learns to say is often 'no'. Sin is everywhere.

Turn on the radio and try to get something educational or cultural and all you will hear are songs about automobiles and money and sex. If it were not for the bad news on the radio, the airwaves would be gloriously silent. It is not a good world we live in. You can become a Protestant, but that does not help much. You can be an American citizen boasting in your Bill of Rights guaranteed in the Constitution and that does not help too much either.

However, when you attach yourself to the Lord of Glory, you are connected with something righteous. He is righteousness itself, and all of the possibility of righteousness is summed up in him. 'But about the Son he says, "Your throne, O God, will last for ever and ever, and righteousness will be the scepter of your kingdom. You have loved righteousness and hated wickedness; therefore God, your God, has set you above your companions by anointing you with the oil of joy"' (Hebrews 1:8–9).

In this mixed-up, confused world we need not despair, for we have a perfectly righteous Saviour. He proved this by his life among the people of his day. During his earthly life and ministry, his enemies spied on him, sending people to search into his life in an attempt to trip him up in something. Can you imagine if Jesus had made a mistake anywhere or lost his temper once? All the sharp beady eyes of hell were following him, trying to catch something damning coming out of his mouth. When the end of his days had almost come, he turned on them and said, 'Which one of you convicts me of sin?' Nobody answered.

Sometime I want to preach a sermon on mercy; I do not think I ever have. Of course, I have woven it into all of my preaching, but have never preached just on the mercy of the Lord Jesus Christ. In the utter mercy of our Lord he sees how bad we are but he is the Lord of all mercy and he does not care. In his great kindness, he takes rebels and unrighteous persons, sinners, makes them his own and establishes them in righteousness and renews a right spirit within them. His righteousness becomes their righteousness and out of chaos comes the divine order. This is the church, a company of believers, and he is their Lord. He is the Lord of all power.

In the New Testament, we have a counterpart to the Song of Songs in the form of Revelation 19:1–5. 'After this I heard what sounded like the roar of a great multitude in heaven shouting: "Hallelujah! Salvation and glory and power belong to our God, for true and just are his judgments. He has condemned the great prostitute who corrupted the earth by her adulteries. He has avenged on her the blood of his servants." And again they shouted: "Hallelujah! The smoke from her goes up for ever and ever." The twenty-four elders and the four living creatures fell down and worshiped God, who was seated on the throne. And they cried: "Amen, Hallelujah!" Then a voice came from the throne, saying: "Praise our God, all you his servants, you who fear him, both small and great."'

This is not hysteria but ecstasy; there is a difference. Hysteria is based on emotion manipulated by exterior stimuli, but ecstasy is based on mystery illuminating the interior part of man's nature. This was ecstasy. It would be worth being put in a salt mine on the Isle of Patmos to have a vision like that.

Years ago, I read one of the greatest books ever written of its kind, *Les Misérables* by Victor Hugo. In it, there was one of the tenderest and most pathetic passages I think I ever read in all literature. You would have to go to the Bible to find things as deeply moving. Here is the story of a young man, one of the upper class of nobles, and the noblewoman he is in love with. Then there is a little urchin girl from the streets of Paris, dressed in rags and with a pale tubercular face. She too loves the nobleman but does not dare say so. The young nobleman uses the young girl to carry notes back and forth to his fiancée and never dreams that this poor sallow-faced girl dressed in rags has lost her heart to him and his nobility. When he discovers this, he goes to find her and see what he can do to help her, and finds her lying in on the bed of rags in a tenement house in the poor area of Paris.

This time she cannot get up to greet him or carry a note to his fiancée. He says to her, 'What can I do for you?'

She tells him, 'I'm dying; I'll be gone in a moment.'

He says, 'What can I do? Tell me; anything.'

And she says, 'Would you do one thing for me before I close my eyes for the last time? Would you, when I am dead, kiss my forehead?'

I know it was only Victor Hugo's brilliant imagination but he had seen that in Paris. He had gone through the sewers, seen this, and knew about it. Hugo knew you could beat a girl down, clothe her in rags, fill her with tuberculosis and make her so thin the wind would blow her off course as she walked down a dirty street. But you could not take out of her heart that thing that made her want to love a man.

God told Adam, 'It is not good for the man to be alone; I will make a helper suitable for him' (Genesis 2:18). And God made woman to be the helpmeet for man; you cannot take that out, and Victor Hugo knew it when he wrote his classic novel. In human nature is planted the desire and need to love.

Our Lord Jesus Christ came down and found the human race like that, consumptive, wan, pale-faced and dying, and he took on himself her death and rose on the third day and took all the pathos out and all the pity out. Now she comes walking, leaning on the arm of her beloved, walking into the presence of God, and he presents her, not a poor pitiful wretch whose forehead he kissed when she was dead but his happy bright-eyed bride, to be partaker with the saints, worthy to stand beside him and be his bride in glory. What is her authority, what is her right, and by what authority does she walk into the presence of God?

I return to that Old Testament illustration. Abraham sent his trusted servant to go and bring back a bride for his son, Isaac. This servant was authorized to bestow jewelry on her as a token from her groom. It was a symbol of his acceptance of her as his bride. Now, how was Isaac going to know his bride? What would set her apart from all other girls? He was going to know her by the jewelry that she had on. He had sent it, and when she came back with it he would recognize her by the jewelry she wore. And so, it says, Isaac took Rebekah and she became his bride.

The Lord of glory sent the Holy Spirit at Pentecost to get a bride, and he will know her by the jewelry she wears.

And what is that jewelry?

For one thing it is the fruit of the Spirit. Love and joy

and peace, kindness and self-control, and all of that. He will know her by what he has bestowed on her. Each of the fruits responds to the nature of Christ. He looks into our life, sees these things that he recognizes as coming from him, and accepts it.

Perhaps the biggest jewel will be that of worship. The bright, shiny, glorious spirit of worship that rests upon the bride of Christ. It is something that is implanted deep in the nature of man. Not all the depravity of human wickedness can destroy that impulse to reach up and out in worship. When God sees that worship, purified by the Spirit and the blood, he responds and recognizes it as his.

Our Lord Jesus Christ will know his bride. He knows who you are and he knows you by the jewelry you wear. 'The king is enthralled by your beauty; honor him, for he is your Lord.'

The poet Jean Sophia Pigott (1845–82) understood this and gave the world the essence of her joy in Christ:

Jesus, I am resting, resting
In the joy of what Thou art;
I am finding out the greatness
Of Thy loving heart;
Thou hast bid me gaze upon Thee,
And Thy beauty fills my soul,
For by Thy transforming power,
Thou hast made me whole.

These are the marks on us that authenticate our belonging to this 'Father of the everlasting ages'.

Prayer:

O God our Father, we thank you for Jesus Christ your Son. We have not done anything that we can think of that does not make us ashamed. We have done so many things of which we ought to be ashamed. We have not done anything ourselves; we have not got anything, our brains, our bodies our souls our spirits, except for what you have given us. What you have given us we are not ashamed of. We are glad for and we are deeply appreciative of your jewels that adorn our lives. Jewels that show the world whose we are. In Jesus' name, Amen.

CHAPTER 13

The Lord of our Worship

1 Peter 2:9

What is the purpose of the local church? And why is the church necessary?

According to the Bible, a local church exists to do corporately what each Christian should do on his or her own. It provides a place in which individual Christians gather together on a Sunday morning and continue to do what we should have been doing all week, namely worshiping God and showing forth the excellence of him who has called us out of darkness into his marvelous light. Reflecting back the glory of him who shone down on us, even God, even Christ, even the Holy Spirit. All that Christ has done for us in the past and all that he is doing now leads to this one end. This is not being taught very much today, that we are saved to worship God. We hear it said that we are saved for a number of reasons.

If you were to ask the average Christian why they were saved, they might respond by referring to peace of mind or to being delivered from smoking or in order to improve their life. If the individual is a businessperson, they might say they took the Lord Jesus on as a helper because they were failing in business and wanted him to be their business partner. We have many reasons, and

I am not going to be too hard on people. In the New Testament, people came to the Lord for many reasons. One man came because his boy was sick. A woman came because her daughter was sick. Another woman came because she had had a chronic disease for twelve years. A politician climbed a tree and looked down because his heart ached and Nicodemus came by night because his religion was not adequate and his heart was empty. But the Lord received them all and the Lord receives everybody that comes to him in faith today, even if their motives may not be the highest.

The point is: why should we always stay where we began? Why should the church be a spiritual school composed of first-graders who never got beyond the first grade? Nobody wants to get any further than this, and I do not mind telling you that I am somewhat sick about this. It seems an awfully badly mixed-up concept of Christianity.

The Lord Jesus Christ died on the cross that he might make his people worshipers of God. That is why we were born, that we might show forth the excellencies of him who has called us out of darkness into his marvelous light. 'Honor him, for he is your Lord.' And we see it when it is all over and the consummation has taken place and been fulfilled. The beasts, the elders and the creatures under the sea, above the earth, in the earth, and in the heavens are all crying aloud, 'Holy, holy, holy is the Lord God Almighty, who was, and is, and is to come' (Revelation 4:8). The purpose of God is that he might redeem us, put us all in the heavenly choir and keep us there singing his praises and showing forth his excellence while the ages roll. This is the purpose of God in redemption.

He has done it for us and is still doing now what he has done; everything leads to one end and all we do should lead to one end. Religious people tend to be very active people, very noisy, wordy and active people. But activity for activity's sake is not of God.

We must bring our ideas into harmony with the Lord of the church. We need to bring our whole thought, our whole philosophy of Christianity, our whole conception of what the church is into harmony with the Lord of the church and his teachings.

I might also say what the church is *not*.

Let us first clear away one misconception: we are not a social club. A church must have certain social commitments and certain fellowship but it is not a social club, and it is not a forum for discussing current events. We read some magazine and then take off like an airplane from a ramp, from what we have just read. We are not a current-events forum and we are not a religious theater providing a place for amateur entertainers to display their talent – home talent, barn talent, or whatever – displaying their gifts. We are none of these things.

We are a holy people, a royal priesthood, a holy generation called out of darkness to show forth the glory of the one who called us out. We should take whatever steps are needed to fulfill our high design as a New Testament church. To do less than this is to fail utterly, to fail God and fail our Lord Jesus Christ who redeemed us.

It is to fail ourselves and it is to fail our children. It is to fail the Holy Spirit who comes from the heart of Jesus to do a work in us. A work that is to be done to make us a holy people, a sanctified people, mirrors of the Almighty to reflect the glory of the most-high God.

Why is this important? For the simple reason that if a local church in one generation fails in its high purpose of worship, the next generation in that church will depart from the faith altogether. That is how liberalism comes about. Many churches stand as a monument to the fact that the generation before failed God, and as a result the present generation succumbs to liberalism and is not preaching the word of God at all. With no Spirit of God upon them and no fire-baptized leaders, they need to compensate. Therefore, they keep it up by social activities and by buying in to whatever is going on in the world. But, as a church, it has failed and is not a church anymore. The glory has departed.

If we could see the visible cloud hanging over churches, which once hung over the camp of Israel in the wilderness, we could easily identify those churches acting in accord with their spiritual nature. If we were permitted to see the fire by night and the cloud by day visibly hanging as a plume over the churches with which God is pleased, I wonder how many churches we would see testifying to the world that they are God's dwelling place? Instead of that, we would see only monuments out in the countryside.

The church must not be accepted as it is or as we find it. We must check it against the word of God and see if this is the way it should be. Then, reverently and quietly, slowly but surely, patiently and lovingly, we bring the church into line with the New Testament to see whether this is the way it would be done if the Holy Spirit were pleased. And when that takes place, the Holy Spirit begins to glow like the lights in the church, and that is what my heart longs to see.

Now, secondly, individual Christians – that is, the individual professed Christian.

Jesus said of the man who was to betray him, 'It would be better for him if he had never been born' (Mark 14:21). And if we fail the purpose for which God created us, then it would be better for us too never to have been born.

How utterly and unspeakably tragic to be forever a broken vase. How utterly tragic that God should make me to be a vase in which he would place the flowers of paradise, the lily of the valley and the rose of Sharon, and out from that simple earthly vessel there would go forth a fragrance that would fill the universe of God. Then I allow that vase to be shattered on the floor and not be used for the purpose God intended. How utterly tragic to be a stringless harp and to have all the shape, outline, and form of a Christian but have no strings that the Holy Spirit could play over. How utterly terrible to be a barren fig tree, with nothing but leaves and no fruit.

Jesus walked out from Jerusalem with his followers and saw a tree; it had leaves on it and he went to that tree and found that it had no figs. The way a fig tree grows is that the fruit comes first and then the leaves.

When the leaves appear in the landscape they tell everybody, 'Come, come, there's fruit here,' as according to the nature of the tree the fruit should have been there before the leaves. But the leaves were there and the order had been reversed, and when Jesus came, parted the leaves, and reached in for figs and there were no figs, he turned to his disciples and said, 'See that tree: no more fruit forever,' and he cursed it and it withered from the top down.

What could be more terrible than to be a barren fig tree, to have the form and delineation of a Christian but bear no fruit. To be a star that does not shine. Think about the dark stars that do not shine and the clouds without rain (Jude 12–13). How terrible to be a shattered mirror of the Almighty, meant by God to catch the beautiful light of God and reflect it back to the entire universe, but instead to be a cracked and shattered mirror that can reflect nothing and thus to be disapproved of by God and banished from the garden, and be eternally aware of all this.

The frightful thing about human beings is our consciousness, that we are aware of things. If it were not for our awareness, nothing could harm us.

The rich man who died and found himself in hell (Luke 16) was conscious that he was there and knew his brothers were not there but would be coming soon. Hell would not be hell if it were not for the consciousness of it. If people slept comatose in hell, it could never be hell.

In the realm of psychology and psychiatry these days the devil is very busy, and has many people who can use phrases they have borrowed from Freud and the rest of them, telling us that we ought not to allow the consciousness of guilt to get us down because that is a guilt complex. We ought not to be too much bothered by religion.

Somebody said to an outstanding head of a great mental institution, after he had been head of that institution for many years, 'Well, doctor, I suppose an awful lot of your patients in here have gone crazy over religion.' He replied, 'To the best of my knowledge, in all the years that I have been head of this institution I have never known one patient that came here because of religion but I have known hundreds that came here that could have been saved from here by religion.'

You ought to thank God if you have a care. I would not take that care away from you at all.

You have to be a purified people if you are going to be worshipers of God, reflecting the image of him who created you. But broken vessels, stringless harps, barren fig trees, clouds without water and cracked mirrors – how tragic and terrible that is.

If you had teeth that were desperately in need of attention, the first thing you would do if you could afford to take a day off from work would be to see a dentist. So how much more important is it that you should find the blood that cleanses you from sin. Nothing should be permitted to hinder us. Friendships – they mean nothing. Business – better to sell peanuts on the street corner than to be caught in a business that grieves the Holy Spirit, breaks the vase, and shatters the mirror. Pleasures – they are for a pleasure-mad people. Rome perished from an overdose of bread and circuses.

Rome, which gave us a language and laws and literature and standards, believed it would never die, yet went down like a great rotten tree. Before whom did Rome go down? It fell to the pagan hordes from the north: the Huns, the Lombards and the rest of the Vandal armies – people unworthy to carry Roman shoes, or even black them. Rome did not die by military conquest from without; Rome died from bread and circuses and pleasure and divorce and fun and too much of everything. It got fat and weak and when it was fat and weak it died.

It is the same way with churches, and the same way with you if you do not look out. It is also the way with countries. I say that nothing should hinder us, not even fear itself, because there is nothing more fearful than failure before God.

What should we do, then? We ought to amend our ways. 'This is what the Lord Almighty, the God of Israel, says: Reform your ways and your actions, and I will let you live in this place. Do not trust in deceptive words and say: "This is the temple of the Lord, the temple of the Lord, the temple of the Lord!"' (Jeremiah 7:3–4). This is our Christian religion. If we thoroughly reform our ways and our actions then God will let us live in this place in the land that he gave our fathers for ever and ever. So let us amend our giving and our praying, our relationships with others, our personal discipline, our prayer lives. Let us amend our ways before God so that we might be a pure people completely acceptable to God, for no pure person can ever be defeated. No pure church can ever perish.

Prayer:

Lord Jesus, we remember your words back then when one of your churches allowed its love to cool off, and you reached down and removed its candlestick for a century and not a trace was left of that church in that city. O Christ, we would seek a perpetual witness before you. We ask that this church would so amend its ways and we should so amend our ways that you can give us a second, a second year, a second decade, a second scroll of years. But until your holy Son comes from heaven the light will shine from this place, not only around our neighborhood but also out to New Guinea and Peru and Brazil and Japan and wherever people need to hear the gospel. O God, we pray you, help us to amend our ways and begin to be and do that for which we were created. Now we are looking to you for help, Lord; we expect you to bless us; we want you to do it. Amen.

CHAPTER 14

Maintaining a Vibrant Worship Lifestyle

Throughout this book, I have maintained that worship is not an event but a lifestyle. The more we treat worship as an event, the more it becomes a caricature of God's intention and unacceptable to him. To maintain a lifestyle of worship we must attend to it on a daily basis. If you regulate worship to a once-a-week event, you really do not understand it and it will take a low priority in your life.

By its nature, worship is not some performance we do but a presence we experience. Unless we have experienced the presence of God in our worship, it cannot rightly be called Christian worship. I have pointed out that there can be worship apart from God, but it is not Christian worship. It is my contention that, once we experience the actual presence of God, we will lose all interest in cheap Christianity with all its bells and whistles vainly trying to compete with the world.

For worship to be a vital part of everyday life, it must be systematically and carefully nurtured.

Let me offer a few suggestions to help along the way. At this point, it is important to steer clear of all those sterile mechanical regimens that think one size fits all. All of us are different and, although we are walking along the same path, we have different personalities. A few essentials need to be a part of our daily walk to maintain a vibrant life of worship. These are a few things that have helped me in my journey along the way with God.

Quietness

I put this first because unless we can find a place without distraction the rest is undermined. We must withdraw from the world and find our repose in God. In such a frantic world as ours, it is almost impossible to find any quietness. Our world is riddled with noise of all kinds and levels of intensity. Not only the world but increasingly the church itself echoes with noise and commotion. Finding a quiet corner to get away to is a great challenge, but well worth it.

When I first became a Christian, it was difficult to find a quiet place. Eventually I found refuge in a corner of our basement where I could focus on worship without interruption. Those were delightful times of fellowship with God and laid the foundation for not only my walk with God but also my ministry in the days to come.

I firmly believe it is important that we become still and wait on God. And it is best that we are alone, preferably with our Bible open before us. I usually have my King James Bible, but I do not think the version is that important. The important thing is to get alone with the word of God. Then in the quietness of the moment and as we draw near to God we will begin to hear him speak in our hearts. This is the most important part of our initial walk with God. To follow God arbitrarily is one thing but I take great pleasure in the scripture that says, 'He who has an ear, let him hear what the Spirit says...' (Revelation 2:11, etc.). The saints of old always followed that voice. They were quiet enough to hear that 'still, small voice of God' speaking to them.

For the average believer the progression will be something like this: first, a sound like that of a presence walking in the garden. Then a voice, more intelligible, but still far from clear. Then the happy moment when the Spirit begins to illuminate the Scriptures, and what has been only a sound, or at best a voice, now becomes an intelligible word, warm, intimate, and clear as the word of a dear friend. Then will come life and light, and, best of all, ability to see and rest in and embrace Jesus Christ as Savior and Lord and All.

The key here is to wait patiently and quietly on God. There is no need to rush. Noise is the enemy of the soul and in our noise-drenched culture it may take some doing, but the result is well worth the effort. Wait until he breaks through the tough exterior of your consciousness.

Cultivating quietness is a missing discipline in today's Christian church. There seems to be a wretched conspiracy in many churches to rob the saints of the quietness necessary to nurture their inner life, which is hidden in Christ in God. The old saints would practice what they called 'tarrying'. They would get on their knees and tarry in God's presence until the light broke into their heart. Sometimes it took all night, but the wait was well worth it.

Scripture

All worship should begin with the Bible. This divine roadmap will lead us to God. It has been a neat trick of the devil to confuse us with a variety of translations. The Christian community is divided by which translation is the right one. I suggest that you settle this matter once for all in your own mind, no matter what it takes, and press on in spiritual growth and maturity. Then put the Bible in a prominent place in your daily life and allow nothing to interfere with reading it and meditating on it.

Our reading here should not be a marathon but a slow, deliberate soaking-in of its message. Bible-reading calendars are no help here. There are times when one verse or even a phrase will strangely appeal to us. It would be impossible to go on until that scripture has done its work in our heart. Do not weaken here. Allow that scripture to marinate in your mind and heart as long as it feeds your soul. God is speaking, and he deserves our utmost respect and attention. Often we restrict ourselves to a daily Bible-reading schedule and hurry on in our reading to keep up. The importance of reading the Bible is not the reading but the fellowship with its author. The proper reading of the Bible must be in the same Spirit that authored it.

I like to memorize portions of Scripture, especially the

psalms of David. Charles Spurgeon used to say that we should read our Bibles until our blood became 'bibline'. I like that. Memorizing the great passages of Scripture will go a long way in meditating on God, especially in the nighttime. 'I have hidden your word in my heart...' the psalmist said (Psalm 119:11), and he knew something of delighting in the presence and fellowship of God.

Prayer

In your prayer life, quickly move beyond the idea of 'getting things' from God. Prayer is not technical in the sense that if we go through the right motions, say the right words, automatically our prayer is answered. Our aim in prayer is not simply 'getting our prayers answered'. Here, we go beyond all that and luxuriate in the overwhelming presence of God. Prayer is not a monologue in which we tell God what we think or want. Rather, it is a dialogue between two friends. An intimate fellowship that more often than not surpasses words. Words can be clumsy and grossly inadequate to express sufficiently how we feel. As the mystics and saints have encouraged, begin practicing the presence of God. This is not merely an exercise in imagination but the ecstatic joy of fellowship. Once you lose yourself in rapturous prayer, you will never go back to prayer by routine.

The key to prayer is simply praying. As we engage with the God of the universe, our hearts are stretched upward in adoring wonder and admiration, resulting in spontaneous worship. Our heart always responds to that heavenly pull. This kind of praying is contagious and thankfully dangerous to the spiritual status quo.

Hymnbook

I must confess that I am an ardent lover of hymns. In my library, I value a collection of old hymnals. Often, on the way to an appointment, I will grab one of these hymnals to read and meditate on. After the Bible, the next most valuable book is a hymnbook. But do not get one that is less than a hundred years old! Let any new Christian spend a year prayerfully meditating on the hymns of Watts and Wesley alone, and he or she will become a fine theologian. Then they should read a balanced diet of the Puritans and the Christian mystics and the result will be more wonderful than you could dream.

The old hymnal is invaluable in my personal walk with God. This may be the most difficult aspect. For a variety of reasons, many have tossed the hymnbook aside or at least ignored it. It has been a successful ploy of the enemy to separate us from those lofty souls who reveled in the rarified atmosphere of God's presence. I suggest you find a hymnbook and learn how to use it. Perhaps one reason the hymnal has fallen out of favor with many is that we do not know how to read or sing a hymn. We are not taught in our churches the great hymns of the church; consequently, many Christians are the poorer, spiritually speaking.

Devotional reading: The mystics and saints

Apart from the Scriptures, which should be paramount in our daily walk with God, some devotional works of bygone saints can help us on our way. I am not thinking of those one-page daily devotionals popular with many people today. They may have some value for those just beginning their spiritual pilgrimage, but the growing Christian needs strong meat. If we are to mature in our Christian experience, we must have food to strengthen us for the journey.

In my search for God, I quite naturally was led to the Christian mystics. As a young Christian, I had never heard of them, nor seen any of their books in the bookstore. A retired missionary thoughtfully placed into my hands one of these old Christian books and I was immediately in love. I discovered that these great saints were uncontrollably in love with God. My love and appreciation for these writers sprang out of my own heart's deep longing after and thirsting for God. These people knew God in a way that I did not and I wanted to know what they knew about God and how they came to know it.

Certainly, in my admiration for these writers, I by no means endorsed everything they did or taught. I early learned that a hungry bee could get nectar out of any old flower and turn it into honey. For me, it was their utter devotion to God along with the ability to share their spiritual insights and observations that I valued. They assisted me in my walk with God as no other writers even of my day have. And, after all, that is all that really matters. I cannot place too much emphasis on the contemplation of divine things, which will result in the God-conscious life. These old mystics did just that for me.

Some have chided me about my affection for some of these old mystic friends of mine. I have learned to rise above that. For me, I require only that a person must know God other than by hearsay. The intricacy of their relationship with God is all that truly matters. If a writer has information to offer that he has obtained only by research, I will pass on him. Give me the writer who has the passion and fire of God in his soul, which flows onto the page.

By mystic, I simply mean that personal spiritual experience common to the saints of Bible times and well known to multitudes of persons in the post-biblical era. I am referring to the evangelical mystics who have been well-versed in the Christian Scriptures. They walk the high road of truth where walked the prophets and apostles of old, and where down the centuries walked martyrs, reformers, Puritans, evangelists and missionaries of the cross. Such people differ from the ordinary orthodox Christian only because they experience their faith down in the depths of their sentient being, while the other does not. They exist in a world of spiritual reality. They are quietly, deeply, and sometimes almost ecstatically aware of the presence of God in their own nature and in the world around them. Their religious experience is something elemental, as old as time, and involves acquaintance with God by union with the eternal Son. It is to know that which passes knowledge.

Simplify your life

The average Christian's life is cluttered with all sorts of activities. We have more going on than we can keep up with and still maintain our inner life with God. Some things need to be rooted out of our daily schedule in order to make room for that one essential thing in our life, the worship of God. Too many things in our life just suck the life out of us and are not essential to wholesome living. We find ourselves rushing through the devotional aspects of our life to give predominance to mere activities. Work without worship is totally unacceptable to God. It would be a good practice to go through your schedule once a month and find one thing to eliminate. Put it on the altar and see how God will respond. It would not be long until the most important thing in your life became your personal worship of God.

Friends/friendships

This area I leave till last because it has the most potential dangers. Your friends will either make or break your deeper walk with Christ. We must carefully choose our friends in this regard. Although it is not necessary to be rude, some friends will need to be marginalized to lessen the damage to our inner life. At times, we are thrown in with friends who are worldly in nature and frivolous in lifestyle. It is easy for our friends to distract us from our walk with Christ and from maintaining a vibrant life of worship. Often we will have to leave our friends behind in order to concentrate on our Friend.

Cultivate friendships with those who have made him who is the Friend of sinners their constant companion.

These simple things will go a long way toward maintaining a vibrant life of worship and praise. If what we believe does not make God more real to us, and make us more Christlike in every aspect of our life, then what value does it have? The maintenance of our worship is a responsibility we cannot shirk. It must be paramount in our daily life. The effect of all this is seen in this verse: 'And we, who with unveiled faces all reflect the Lord's glory, being transformed into his likeness with ever-increasing glory, which comes from the Lord, who is the Spirit' (2 Corinthians 3:18).

May God grant us all a desire for himself that supersedes all other desires.

Prayer:

Dear heavenly Father, the world is very evil, times are waxing late and we are running out of time. O God, take hold of us. We pray that we may have eyes to see and ears to hear and hearts to understand. We pray that we may be saved from routine and rut. We pray that we may have eyes inside and outside, and an anointed understanding. Help us, Lord, for Christ's sake. Amen.